HANNAH IN AMERICA

HANNAH IN AMERICA

HANNAH HAUXWELL
with BARRY COCKCROFT

Principal photographs by Mostafa Hammuri

TED SMART

Also by Barry Cockcroft
Hannah in Yorkshire
The Ways of a Yorkshire Dale
The Dale that Died
Princes of the Plough
A Romany Summer
A Celebration of Yorkshire
Seasons of My Life
Daughter of the Dales
Hannah: The Complete Story
Innocent Abroad
Hannah's North Country

A TED SMART Publication 1994

First published 1993

First published in the United Kingdom in 1993 by Century Limited
Random House, 20 Vauxhall Bridge Road, London SW1V 2SA

Random House Australia (Pty) Limited
20 Alfred Street, Milsons Point, Sydney,
New South Wales 2061, Australia

Random House New Zealand Limited
18 Poland Road, Glenfield
Auckland 10, New Zealand

Random House South Africa (Pty) Limited
PO Box 337, Bergvlei, South Africa

Random House UK Limited Reg. No. 954009

Design by Behram Kapadia
Filmset by SX Composing Ltd, Rayleigh, Essex
Printed and bound by Gráficas Estella, S. A.

ISBN 0 09 178783 1

Contents

Preface

Uncle Sam the Cowboy

Uncle Sam and the cowboys – that's always been my vision of America and I cannot imagine it will change. I think of Uncle Sam as a person, big in every way – physically and mentally. Friendly, jolly, and kind too. A countryman, perhaps even a cowboy.

I have built this image in my mind from a very young age in the same way as most people, I suppose: from reading cowboy books and going to the cinema on the few occasions that was possible. Uncle Tommy, who came to look after Low Birk Hatt farm after my father, his brother, died at a very young age, was very fond of cowboy books. He borrowed from the library and sometimes from neighbours, so literature was my first introduction to America. I read a lot, and I was particularly impressed by Zane Gray's stories because he could describe the countryside so vividly, as well as the action. One of his characters caught my imagination. He was called Nevada. He came riding by one day and was given hospitality by this young couple who were experiencing some real troubles. A group of very unpleasant characters were trying to take their land from them. So he stayed to help them, took care of things and then he just rode away. He was Nevada when he came, and Nevada when he left, and nothing else. I really liked him.

Later on, the cinema brought America to life in a more direct way. I didn't see many films before the war because Baldersdale was so isolated and transport almost non-existent. Then they began to run a bus on a Saturday evening right to

Cowboy Country.

the top of the Dale. So I was able to go a few times to Barnard Castle where two cinemas thrived: the Scala and the Victoria (which was a converted chapel). Gene Autry was the first cowboy I ever saw, and then Roy Rogers came along with his lovely horse, Trigger. Randolph Scott was another favourite of mine – he was such an admirable man, with nice strong features. I think I preferred him to John Wayne.

They were very enjoyable films and, like the books, good usually triumphed over evil. That, unfortunately, doesn't always happen in real life but it's as well to have that end in view. I tried my best to make the first house of the cinema because of the bus timetable. The second house wasn't such a happy affair because you had to watch the clock, since the bus back to Baldersdale left at a quarter past ten, sharp. I would stay until the last possible moment and then have to rush, but I still missed the end of the film on several occasions. Uncle never went with me to the cinema so I assume he was happy with his books, but he was even more enthusiastic about cowboys than me. I suppose we both identified somewhat with the cowboy because we lived and worked on the land – in a different way, of course, but we still had horses and cattle at Low Birk Hatt farm, and ours was something of a frontier community! Very lawful, naturally, but isolated and largely self-supporting. Yorkshire is Britain's Texas, you know, with lots of space and a certain sense of wildness. Indeed, for years one of my favourite phrases to describe a trustworthy person has been 'someone you can ride the river with', because herding cattle across a river has always been a very tricky business and you have to choose very carefully the people to go with. And your horse.

At Low Birk Hatt, 1972.

Then there is the cowboy music which I enjoy very much – they could sing and play just as well as they could ride and shoot. Uncle and I never missed Big Bill Campbell and his Rocky Mountain Rhythm on the wireless, but that was many years ago. I even saw the man himself once, when he came to a theatre in Darlington. It's possible he and his fellow artists had never been anywhere near the American West, but I suppose it's better not to know. I played one of Big Bill's records when I did a Christmas show on the radio last year.

Anyway, as I write this on my way to America, I consider myself very fortunate indeed. I have always had good feelings about the place and never really understood the anti-American sentiments which some people express. They even say their bad weather lands in Britain!

Now I haven't met many Americans up to now, but those I have have impressed me very favourably indeed, contrary to the popular view that they are brash and boastful and loud. The first American I ever knew was the late Mr Norman Field, who was related to the Marshall Field store family in Chicago. He owned Lartington Hall, one of the big houses in Teesdale, was a Master of Hounds, and a very grand and important person. But he was very pleasant to me on the few occasions I spoke with him. A real gentleman.

In more recent times I have made some very good American friends, particularly a couple from Houston in Texas, called John and Kathleen Stone. It must be fifteen years since they first turned up on my doorstep in Baldersdale. They were living in Britain at the time and had seen the first film about me, *Too Long a Winter*. Such a likeable pair, quiet and modest and charming. They were in the oil business and I assume they are retired now. They kept in touch with me, and I once had a letter from them posted in Saudi Arabia. We plan to go to Houston on this trip, but, unfortunately, I have misplaced their address. It would be so good to see them once again, but I don't know how to find them.

Years ago, Uncle and I often used to say that if the chance to travel abroad ever happened, he and I would part company at the farm gate, with me going east to Paris and him west to America to look for cowboys.

It's sad in a way. I got my chance to go to Paris and many other wonderful European cities when my *Innocent Abroad* television series was made in 1991. Now I am on my way west.

So I'll be going for the both of us.

1

First Leg – Towards the Ultimate Ship

The entire village seemed to know what was afoot. I do lead a rather public life these days and the newspapers had been writing stories about my proposed tour of America, despite all efforts to keep it quiet. Mind, Cotherstone is such a warm and friendly place, and all manner of good friends and neighbours popped in to wish me well and enquire as to whether I had remembered to get my travel sickness pills. Leaving my little dog, Timmy, is always a problem, particularly on lengthy trips like this one. Putting him into boarding kennels, however good, does worry me. But there was the answer to this particular maiden's prayer when a lady I met three years ago at a church in Wolsingham, about ten miles from Cotherstone, asked about my plans for Timmy. Miss Jesse Pickering is her name, and we hit it off from the moment we were introduced. She volunteered to look after him for me, which was such a blessing.

Kelvin Walker, our local garage proprietor and taxi driver, drove me to Darlington Railway Station as usual and there was quite an emotional moment for me when I was standing on the platform. I saw the yellow engine of the London train appearing around the corner and I had such strange feelings. Excitement, of course, because I was off on the first leg of a trip to what for me was the other side of the world, but it also brought home to me that I was leaving good people behind for a long, long time. I knew I would meet no one better than them.

Start of a stroll down Piccadilly.

TDK
AUDIO & VIDEO TAPE
SANYO
H.SAMUEL
THE EXPERIENCE OF
MADAME TUSSAUDS

The reality of the occasion suddenly dawned, I suppose, and I waved to Kelvin for as long as I could see him.

The train was very quiet, and I relished the peace of the journey after all the turmoil of preparation and packing. My dear friend Kathy Rooney helped me to buy new clothes and sort out my three pieces of luggage – I'm hopeless on my own when it comes to decisions of that sort.

There are certain problems with me and clothes. I don't like stockings, so skirts are not always practical; but it's the matter of underwear that really bothers me. I've been left behind the times, I'm afraid, because I like bloomers, with elastic at the waist and just above the knee, and have always worn them. I do not understand how ladies of even larger proportions than me get into the modern underwear. Everything today seems to be geared to people with slender figures, and I have put on a bit of weight since I retired from the farm. Almost a stone in fact.

I landed in London to a real surprise. Barry Cockcroft, Mostafa Hammuri and Chris Greaves, the same team who went with me on my grand tour of Europe for the *Innocent Abroad* series and book were all waiting on the platform to greet me. Another big moment, but this time all pleasurable. That's when the excitement really started. It's just as well someone was there because I had no idea how to move around London on my own. I stick to a certain policy: if there is nobody to meet me, I stay put on the platform until somebody does turn up. My second option would be to go to the Lost Property office!

After checking into the Mayfair Hotel, I had a sentimental stroll down Piccadilly (I do so love visiting our capital city), and called at Hatchards, the bookshop that counts the Royal family among its clients. They had filled one window with a display of my books, a much appreciated honour.

The new two days were spent putting the finishing touches to our travel plans at Messrs Thomas Cook's splendid premises just off Piccadilly. They had handled all the arrangements for the European trip, so I was among friendly and familiar faces. I spent an afternoon chatting to a real expert in global travel, a remarkable gentleman called Edmund Swinglehurst who heads the Archive section of Thomas Cook's, and is an author to boot. Such an interesting and varied life he has led – born in Chile, he once spent a while as an artist in Paris where he worked alongside famous painters such as Matisse. Apparently he had a difficult time financially – not an unusual situation for

Hatchards – a window full of my books.

Afternoon tea with Edmund Swinglehurst.

artists, I gather – but he was offered a job by Cook's because he could speak fluent Spanish and the package holiday business was beginning to boom. He never left, and is now a very important member of staff, and looks very youthful for a man born in 1917.

We finished the meeting over afternoon tea at the Mayfair Hotel, a most elegant place. I'd stayed there once before, when Thomas Cook's invited me to present their Travel Book of the Year Award – to an American gentleman as it happened. That's when I first made Mr Swinglehurst's acquaintance.

Next day we drove down to Southampton in glorious sunshine to prepare to leave Britain in style. I tend to go for the very top when I do things these days. The first hotel I ever stayed in was the London Savoy, then I came home from Europe on the Orient Express, and now here I was, about to cross the Atlantic for the first time on the most famous ship in the world.

The QE2.

I knew it was a big ship, but my first glimpse quite took my breath away. I stood at the front end – the bow, I believe they call it – and looked up. It seemed to rise for ever. It was truly huge. Getting on board was a bit of a pantomime, with ramps and escalators and all kinds of security checks. This was the first time I had been obliged to offer my handbag for X-ray examination and then step through a metal doorway, which checked for weapons and other dangerous items on the person. There was a bit of confusion when a lady official questioned me about my luggage – whether I had packed it myself and had anybody given me anything to bring with me. Well, Kathy Rooney had helped me to pack and I was trying to answer to the best of my ability when the lady dissolved into laughter. It seemed she recognised me, so all was well.

Eventually we all finished up in a lounge and at first I thought we had boarded, but I was wrong. It was yet another building alongside the QE2. We had to wait for a long time for more document inspections before being allowed through yet another set of doors, which finally led us to the reception desk.

The Ultimate Ship.

Then all the frustration and confusion vanished. I was guided to my cabin, which turned out to be one of the first class category. I certainly never expected it to be so big and luxurious; there was even a bottle of Champagne and a basket of fruit, including a bowl of strawberries, on the sideboard. I enjoyed the fruit, and the Champagne went to where it was appreciated! Then it was back on deck to watch the farewell

ceremonies, with people crowding the railings and waving to what I presume were relatives and friends on shore, and the band of the Royal Welsh Fusiliers playing us away as we drifted slowly from the dockside.

On our way!

Back in my cabin I watched through the porthole as good old England slowly receded, which was another sentimental moment. People may think me silly, but I consider occasions like that should be thought about, if only privately. I had been

Aboard the QE2.

very touched by a card and a teddy bear sent as a surprise to the ship from my good friends at Abbot Hall in Grange-over-Sands, which I often visit. I also tried (but failed) to spot the Isle of Wight along the way, because some people connected with the chapel there had invited me to visit and I would like to go.

Anyway, I settled down to start life at sea for five days and nights on the QE2. It's hard to get over in words just how vast this boat is. When I stood outside my cabin door and looked at the corridor stretching as far as the eye could see in either direction, it occurred to me that a three-wheeled bike would come in handy – I am not much good on the two-wheeled sort. Fortunately, I always had Barry, Mostafa or Chris to guide me round the boat. I am sure that if I had been let loose on my own I would never have been seen again. I met one poor old lady in the lift who had been going up and down in confusion for quite a long time, trying to locate where she should be. There are lifts everywhere, and I counted eleven decks. The ship was much like a town with all the streets piled on top of each other. My fellow passengers seemed to be rather well off – even wealthy,

judging from their clothes and jewellery – so I was a mite worried how they would react to a simple soul like me when I turned up for dinner on the first night. But they proved to be remarkably friendly, particularly some Americans sitting at tables close by. They were from New York, and when they found out I was staying in that city (which they did within minutes) I was showered with advice about where to go and what to see and what to eat. They were particularly keen for me to visit a certain steakhouse, which they agreed amongst

Afternoon refreshments.

themselves was the best in the world, and also urged me to try soft shell crabs. Apparently you eat the lot, shells and all, which seemed very curious to me. As it happens, we were being offered some truly exotic food as we conversed, such as Russian caviar, lobsters cooked in a variety of ways and several dishes flamed rather alarmingly in spirits like brandy. I rose quickly from my seat and moved away when they lit one bonfire immediately behind me, which caused a bit of a stir. But everyone was good humoured about it.

Personally I stick to eating what I am familiar with – plain fish, well cooked meat and bread rolls, which were delicious. I have a mind to try lobster one day, when the occasion is right and no alcohol is involved in the sauce.

But I ate next to nothing the second day out, because I foolishly forgot my travel sickness tablets. A bit of a swell had developed when we began to steam out into the Atlantic and I spent most of the day in my bed, but I had to stir myself in the evening because I was one of a group due to be presented to the master of the ship. Now, one can foresee a few problems as you go through this life, but I never thought the captain of the QE2 would be one of them, in the sense that I was feeling poorly and having to get ready for a formal occasion, which I always dread at the best of times because I am invariably frightened of doing or saying the wrong thing. And to cap it all, I was also to be presented to the captain's wife, an unusual honour.

Captain and Mrs John Burton-Hall proved to be charm itself, and we chatted for several minutes as a long queue waited to follow me. Then Rosemarie Burton-Hall, a very elegant and beautiful lady in a dress to match, whisked me away into a quiet corner of the grand lounge for a long and friendly conversation. There were to be many similar chats with any number of people in the days that followed. I suppose I am gradually getting over the surprise of being recognised and greeted by so many people, but I didn't imagine it would

Meeting Captain and Mrs Burton-Hall.

happen on the QE2 like it does on the streets back home. But it is very gratifying, however, and I am making so many friends.

During our meeting, the captain invited me to visit the bridge the following day, and what an exciting experience that proved to be. I had to climb with my escort to the top of the ship to see what the captain proclaimed to be the very best view of the North Atlantic, and so it was. What an important and responsible job the captain of the QE2 has, with around three thousand passengers and crew to deliver safely across a perilous ocean. And what a striking figure Captain Burton-Hall made as he stood in full uniform at his command post. He had a classic seaman's full beard, and an unmistakable air of authority. And to prove just how unpredictable sea journeys can be even in the best of hands, we collided with a whale one day and the engines had to be stopped to enable officers to inspect the bow for any damage. The captain said over the public address system that the whale must have been dead or very sick. Because the QE2 made such a noise underwater, no self-respecting whale would have been within a mile of the ship.

During my visit to the bridge I was quite taken by an array of naval officers' hats hanging on pegs alongside the various

A visit to the bridge.

Ready to take up duty!

banks of navigational and steering devices. Apparently, it is customary for an officer to reach for his hat and put it on to signify that he is taking up his duties on the bridge. The captain told me that the QE2 was not a cruise ship, but the last of the super liners and the only one capable of crossing the North Atlantic at a steady speed of more than thirty miles an hour.

I was then privileged to be taken down to the captain's luxurious quarters on the deck immediately below the bridge, where Rosemarie Burton-Hall was waiting. Over a cup of tea – served by the captain, no less – she told me about how they had met and married. It was a real fairy story romance. They saw each other for the first time on the QE2, when she was a member of a theatre group performing plays on board. It had happened twelve years previously when he was the staff captain of the QE2, and she actually had a photograph of their very first meeting. As it happened, he was one of the few officers she had not met up to then – and she had been on board for some time. It was the night of the captain's reception, but fog had descended on the North Atlantic and the captain was obliged to remain on the bridge. So Staff Captain John Burton-Hall was deputising. Mrs Burton-Hall told me that when she found out it was 'only the staff captain', she thought it wouldn't be worth while to bother to dress up and come down for the ceremonial handshake. She said that her indifference even showed in her face on the photograph taken of their meeting. They met again a few days later – and within twenty minutes were planning to get married! She said she had never met anyone else who could beat that time.

Apparently, Cunard are very considerate towards the wives of their senior officers, and Mrs Burton-Hall was able to sail with him for most of his tours of duty, which generally cover around eight months of the year. She obviously loved travelling the world in such style, but I noticed that she worked very hard alongside him at the numerous social events the captain had to attend. She said that life on board a liner was very similar to being a member of a theatre group – you become almost as close as a family for a short period of time. And she thought it most important for every passenger to feel a similar warmth, since for many it was a once-in-a-lifetime experience for which they had probably planned and saved for years.

I met a charming young man who was a rising young officer, like his captain had been twelve years before, and – small world – he turned out to come from Barnard Castle, which is just a few miles down the road from my home. Ian McNaught was his name, and he was keen to introduce himself to a fellow Teesdalian. Now living in Washington, near Durham – he told me the American Washington was the imitation one – he had been at sea for twenty-one years, and joined Cunard in 1986. Ian told me he was a qualified master mariner, like all the first officers on the QE2, but he was a Senior First Officer, which put him very close to the top. He said it was likely he would have been master of his own vessel by now if he had stayed with another shipping line, but promotion with Cunard was very slow and he expected it may have been another ten years before he was given his own command. However, he was happy to wait, because the lifestyle was superior with Cunard.

I knew exactly what he meant. You certainly live a very full life on the QE2. There seemed to be some activity going on in every corner of every deck, and there must have been dozens of musicians, dancers and singers on board performing night and day. Considering my weakness for music in all its forms,

Ian McNaught – fellow Teesdalian.

that was the chief attraction for me. Talks and lectures on all manner of subjects were frequent and you could even have dancing lessons, which was something I rather fancied since I never did learn to dance. But I was too busy to try because they had arranged two book-signing sessions for me, which were quite lengthy occasions (the librarian said they were the most successful in her experience), then I had to do something called 'An Afternoon with Hannah Hauxwell' in the big theatre. As fate would have it, I was competing with the Captain, who was giving a talk and answering questions at the same time in another part of the ship. We discussed this matter during our meeting on the bridge and both thought it unfortunate – I would have loved to have listened to him because he was such a grand speaker.

I was very kindly received by a large audience, including a fair number of Americans. Barry Cockcroft came on stage first to describe how he first met me, and showed a short excerpt from one of my documentaries. Then he introduced me. We talked for a while, and then invited questions from the audience. I have done several sessions of this nature before –

INNOCENT ABROAD

A successful signing session.

even appeared on theatre stages in various parts of the country – but not, I think, with the same poise and confidence of our captain's wife. I am always surprised and gratified at the affectionate interest shown by audiences in my past activities and future plans. The questions generally follow a similar pattern, and a sample of those asked by my fellow passengers on the QE2 goes like this:

Clearly, it's a marvellous life you are leading now, but where is your heart?

Oh, a lot of me is in the old house, but life moves on. I stayed as long as I could, as long as it was wise and possible to do so. It's no good having animals and not being able to look after them. You cannot live in the past, and I have enjoyed life during the four years since I left Low Birk Hatt and look forward, God willing, to the future.

Do you ever go back to Low Birk Hatt?

No, and I don't know whether I will ever be able to. If I did and became homesick then that would be it – the rest of my life would be a misery. It's better just to live with my memories.

Where did you move to, and what are the main differences to life in an isolated dale?

Well, I only travelled six miles to the village of Cotherstone, but it was still a big adventure for me. I was lucky because there were several people there who had lived in Baldersdale in the past, even someone I'd been to school with, and they all rallied round magnificently to make me welcome. And I like my cottage and all the amenities such as water on tap and central heating, which I didn't have at Low Birk Hatt. But it was a big change. It's really a matter of space . . . I'm accustomed to having space around me, and my new home is on the main road and only has a small garden at the front. I remember my first Easter in Cotherstone. I had been for a walk with my little dog and was trying to cross the road to my cottage. The traffic was very heavy, the place was crowded with people, I had started my first cold for many years . . . and I wondered what on earth I was doing there! But that feeling has passed. These days, of course, I am so busy I am away from home quite a lot.

Appearing on stage with Barry Cockcroft.

Had you any particular plan for the future in mind – such as retirement – before television changed everything?

No, I hadn't. I knew I would have to do something about retirement one day, but I was just too busy with the animals to think about it.

You were on your own at the farm with no telephone – what would have happened if you had become seriously ill or suffered an accident?

Yes, well I know my good friends used to worry about that. But I rarely thought about it except, maybe, when I was climbing the ladder to the byre top at night without a light. If I had fallen I could have been lying there a good while. But there was always the postman, and the hikers coming along the Pennine Way, which ran through my land. The risk was worse in winter, of course, when the snow made even a short distance seem a long way, particularly if you were taken poorly. That reminds me – someone once asked me if I had ever considered acquiring a deep freeze to store food since the shops were so far away, and I said that I didn't need a deep freeze because I lived in one!

When you were on your own did you take any precautions about your safety, such as keeping a gun under your bed?

No, although someone once said that I should. I said I would be more likely to shoot myself than anybody else! But the farm was well away from the road and if some crackpot had taken it into his mind to find it he would not have found it easily. As a matter of fact, it is probably more necessary to worry about security in a village like Cotherstone than my old place in Baldersdale.

Why do people think so much of you, and how do you cope with being recognised wherever you go?

I have absolutely no idea why people are so affectionate towards me. It's a mystery, because I am very ordinary. As for being recognised and approached, I don't really mind. In fact, its very nice – flattering, really. Sometimes it creates a problem if I am rushing somewhere for a train or an appointment, but generally I welcome the kindness.

I could have gone on for much longer that we did, but another event was scheduled after us, and our time ran out. I finished by reading 'The Teesdale Hills' by Richard Watson, our local poet, who lived in the nineteenth century. It all went very well, to my enormous relief.

The voyage was an entirely happy one, apart from the spell of seasickness which was soon cured when I took the medication, and ended in spectacular fashion as we approached New York. I am not an early riser, but for this

The QE2 approaches New York.

occasion I was quite happy to leave my bed at 4 a.m. to go to the top deck, which was already crowded by the time I arrived.

It was a beautiful dawn. Indeed, some of the QE2's officers who had made this voyage many times rated it the best they had ever seen. There was one quite dramatic moment when we approached an enormously long bridge, and it seemed the funnel was going to collide with it. It was an optical illusion of course, but there was an audible sigh of relief and a round of applause when we steamed safely under.

Then there was the thrill of my first sight of the Statue of Liberty. It crossed my mind what a welcome sight this must have been to many thousands of people fleeing from persecution and poverty in times gone by. The Manhattan skyline began to grow in the morning mists with the sun

Dawn on deck.

The Manhattan skyline.

peeping rosily between the skyscrapers. All the cameras worked overtime, including ours.

When Thomas Cook's son was setting up the first excursion to the New World he was amazed by what he called the beauty of New York harbour, with 'all the green trees and little Swiss-type wooden houses'! He wouldn't have recognised it today. No trees in view, unfortunately. I was a bit apprehensive about how a country bumpkin like me would cope with all the noise and those daunting buildings, but we had arrived and the adventure was about to begin!

2

New York, New York – But Why the Big Apple?

As it happened, we got off to a slow start in New York. It was a long job disembarking from the QE2, waiting in line for customs and immigration inspections, and then the large minibus which should have been waiting for us on the dockside didn't materialise. Mostafa and Chris went off into the streets to find a taxi and track it down. Barry and I were left on the pavement in a less than attractive area, guarding twenty-five pieces of equipment and luggage worth goodness knows how many thousands of pounds. Two hours later we were still there, in ninety degrees of heat, and half choked by the exhaust fumes of enormous lorries driving past within inches and carrying provisions to the QE2. That was coming down to earth with a thump after all the luxury we had indulged in during the previous five days.

On closer inspection New York proved to be fascinating – not as formidable as I had expected. Those buildings! I cannot imagine how they ever got them built or how they ever keep standing up, they are so high. I was also much taken by the people on the streets. I have never seen such a variety, all colours, shapes and sizes. And the clothes they wore – remarkable. Despite the crowds, I found it reasonably comfortable to walk along the streets because the pavements were so wide, they are even easier to negotiate than those in London. I did encounter a problem at the crossing places, because vehicles start coming at you from the side even when the 'Don't Walk' sign has changed to 'Walk'. They won't give

End of the voyage.

you a minute, and it was necessary to nip smartly along the last few yards. I wondered how old folk and the disabled managed.

I was taken on a tour of Fifth Avenue, which is full of exclusive and very expensive shops, and entered an extraordinary building called Trump Tower, which was mostly gold in colour with lovely pink marble floors and a waterfall down one wall. But I didn't get further than the ground floor because the only way up was by escalator. I don't like escalators at the best of times. I can usually manage the British variety, but this one was going so fast – somewhat typical of the pace of life in New York, I imagine. I had a try, but it frightened me so much that I had to jump off. It took me several minutes to recover.

I was much happier out on the streets window shopping. I came across Tiffany's, the famous jewellery store, but it was nothing like I expected. Quite a disappointment, really. The windows were tiny and only one piece of jewellery was displayed in each. Apparently they were all precious stones, but I wouldn't know the difference between diamonds and

On guard, with twenty-five pieces of luggage and equipment.

Entering Trump Tower.

A welcome at the Plaza.

glass. It occurred to me that Young's, the Jewellers in Barnard Castle, had more to show in their windows than Tiffany's.

But our hotel in New York was something very special. I have stayed in some very wonderful places during my travels, and, although the Savoy in London will always have a particular place in my affections, the Plaza in New York was magnificent. I thought it was like Buckingham Palace, which I did enter briefly once when attending the Queen's Garden Party – in at one door and out of the next. The Plaza had the same kind of grandeur, with enormous chandeliers and ornate ceilings. The sitting room of my suite was five times the size of the average British hotel room, with windows overlooking Central Park and Fifth Avenue. They were double glazed, too, but still you could hear the roar of the city, punctuated regularly by the piercing police car sirens. And sometimes I fancied I could hear a ship in the distance, as though the QE2 was calling me back!

Just one corner of my luxury suite.

The people working in the hotel were extremely courteous and very interested in me and why I was there, and the quality of service was quite outstanding – with one exception.

Tea.

I thought that America would be more civilised when it came to making a pot of good tea, but even in the Plaza there was no improvement on the continental system of bringing a jug of hot water and a tea-bag for you to make it yourself. Inevitably, by the time it got to you the water was well off the boil. As everyone knows, I am addicted to tea, and I had expected that because of the British influence, and since America used to belong to us and millions of Americans have British blood in their veins, I would not encounter the problems I faced during my tour of Europe.

I'm afraid America urgently needs educating when it comes to tea making.

One evening my kind gentleman companions took me on a walk through the streets because they wanted me to try a meal at a place they call a deli, of which New York has an

. . . but the tea was disappointing (*above*). Fifth Avenue (*right*).

abundance. They are unusual places, very busy, but very friendly and relaxing. Indeed, I did something I have never done in a public place before – took off my shoes and sat in my stockinged feet. Such a relief after all that walking through the hot streets. The menu read like a foreign language and I had no idea what we ate (even my companions could only guess), but it tasted fine. The portions were enormous. Each plate was piled with enough to feed the average family in my estimation. The one sad part of an otherwise fascinating walk was the sight of numerous poor people, mainly black, on every street holding out plastic cups and begging for your change. There seems to be this contrast in all the big cities, with extreme wealth rubbing shoulders with abject poverty. Many rich folk seem to travel around in what they call stretch limos, which were more than twice the length of what we consider to be big cars in Britain, and looked as if they were about to sag in the middle. They looked large enough to live in, and I was told they had telephones, television sets and even cocktail cabinets.

We saw one unpleasant instance on that walk, when two taxis had a minor collision. New York taxi drivers do seem to drive very recklessly and so accidents must be frequent. A noisy row broke out but I couldn't understand what they were saying, which was probably just as well. There is a vague atmosphere of violence in certain New York streets and to judge by the frequent wail of sirens, the police are kept very busy. I understand there are far too many guns about in the United States, and to my mind that also applies to the police. I saw a group of about twenty officers, all armed, walking together through the hotel (President Clinton was in New York that day), and one or two of them looked very young and maybe not yet responsible enough to carry a gun.

I do know with certainty just what New York is short of – trees. All those long streets and avenues and scarcely a bit of greenery, until you arrive at Central Park, that is. They seem to concentrate all their trees in that one spot, and grateful the New Yorkers must be for that lovely place. A young lady guide from the tourist office kindly accompanied me on a horse-and-buggy ride through Central Park, and it proved to be big enough to escape the clamour of the streets. You could hear the birds at last. The park spreads over 850 acres and was full of people enjoying themselves, particularly the youngsters who raced along in numbers on a kind of roller skate I'd never seen before, with rubber wheels in a line instead of one at each

An equestrian friend – Plaza in the background.

corner. We passed a very attractive lake, and I was shown a sad place called Strawberry Fields, created in memory of John Lennon and situated just opposite the apartment block where he was shot and killed. My guide told me that his widow, Yoko Ono, still lived there.

She was a fund of knowledge about the city, so I took the opportunity to try and ascertain the correct answer to a certain question. My neighbour in Cotherstone, Dave Warry, asked me to find out why New York was called the 'Big Apple'. I had asked a couple of friends on the QE2, and they said a previous mayor of New York had described it as a big apple that

A carriage ride in Central Park.

everyone could enjoy; but my guide said it originated among jazz musicians in New Orleans. They considered New York to be the apex of their profession, the Big 'A', and they all wanted to work there. Well, maybe Big A evolved into Big Apple. But I was left with a feeling that neither explanation seemed to fit.

Central Park was very hot that day and I was somewhat concerned about the horses pulling the carriages. Our driver was a friendly chap with an interesting story to tell. He was an Irishman who had come over on a visit ten years previously but never went back. I thought he used the whip rather more than

Flowers in the park.

necessary, and I saw no water or food provided for the horse, even when they were back at his station. And then at night I saw the horses still out, yoked up to their carriages with their owners still plying for business. Not one of them had anything to drink, nor any fodder. I recall that when Tom Parker, the cart man who brought the provisions into Baldersdale when I was young, always had with him a big string net full of hay so the horse could eat whenever he stopped to unload.

I just wish they would do the same for the horses in New York.

3

Proclaim Liberty Throughout All the Land . . . My Meeting with the Amish

The next step in my journey across America was concerned with Liberty. We drove along the East Coast to Philadelphia, not the most romantic of cities but without a doubt the very spot where this comparatively young nation began, more than two hundred years ago. It is regrettable in a way that this event had to be achieved after an unpleasant conflict with Great Britain, but that is all in the past now.

There is a bell in Philadelphia which was cast from two thousand pounds' weight of bronze in London in 1753, and became the symbol of freedom for many causes down the centuries. First, it rang to celebrate the cutting loose of America from Britain, when the Declaration of Independence was first read out in public on 8 July 1776, in Philadelphia. Today it stands in a special pavilion in front of Independence Hall, and one and a half million people come to see it each year. I joined the queue myself and discovered that it wouldn't ring any more because it was badly cracked. They had trouble with it from the very first, which doesn't say much for the bellmakers of London. But the guide who explained its history said that some people say it rings louder than ever. It was certainly a blessed sound to the thousands who fled oppression in Europe and elsewhere as the young nation opened its gates to everyone. 'Proclaim Liberty Throughout all the Land' says the inscription on the bell, and that also meant freedom to follow whatever religious beliefs you wished. It was a very welcome message to one particular group of people whose strict code of

The Liberty Bell.

LAND UNTO
PROVINCE OF

life and peculiar dress makes them the object of constant curiosity from the general public.

The Amish.

Now America is as modern a place as you will find in all the world, I imagine, but when you travel a few miles into Pennsylvania from Philadelphia and enter a place called Lancaster County, you could believe you had travelled back in time to the last century and even beyond. For that is where the Amish established themselves and held fast to their customs and beliefs. They are farming folk who are immediately recognisable by their unusual dress – severe black suits for the men, long skirts and bob caps for the ladies, since it seems the heads must be covered at all times, even the children's. The men wear broad-brimmed black hats for best, and straw ones for working. They will not have anything to do with electricity, or use motor-propelled vehicles of any kind; they work the land with horses and light their homes with kerosene lamps

The good earth of Amish country.

A bridge with a roof.

and candles. I have to confess that I lived something of an Amish life myself for many years in Baldersdale, but not through choice.

Lancaster County was very rural, and dotted with little towns named in the most curious fashion. You could visit Paradise, if you wish! And Bird in Hand, Intercourse or Strasburg. And down every narrow lane you could see half a dozen of those strange, black, horse-drawn buggies, totally enclosed and usually driven by an old, white-bearded man. I spent hours watching the Amish working the fields, and saw mules for the first time in my life. I had only read about them before, since there were no mules in Baldersdale, and rather strange creatures they were, with those long, pointed ears. And do those Amish work, man and beast. I saw many teams of six mules or horses with only one man controlling them. They toiled from dawn to dusk, and judging from the intense effort required for that type of farming, they must go to bed exhausted.

The Amish women have plenty to do as well, because large families are commonplace, and I noticed washing lines up to fifty feet in length full of heavy, sombre clothes hung out to dry. I do not know how they manage, without the help of electricity, to wash and cook for so many. However, they still find the time to stitch the most attractive quilts and I was taken to see one being made. We did quilting in our family but

nothing to match their skill, which I believe is world famous.

Quilt making the Amish way.

I was fascinated to spend an hour watching a lady working on an enormous quilt with a beautiful design. She was wearing a mop cap, Amish style, but was not Amish herself although she had learned from friends and neighbours who were. She said it was a tradition which had been thriving in Lancaster County for around two hundred years. Naturally, it was all done by hand.

She had already spent two months sewing away on that quilt and estimated that it would take another two weeks to finish. I told her it would take me two years, even if I was capable. I was shown the templates to work out a design, on sale to those who wanted to try themselves, but I resisted the temptation. I spend quite a lot of my spare time sewing, whenever my eyes will permit, but I couldn't hope to achieve the standard this lady was setting. Nor did I consider taking one home with me, because the asking price for the one she was sewing was somewhere between seven hundred and nine hundred dollars.

She demonstrated how it was done – stitching two pieces of cloth together with a 'batting' of a thin polyester material inserted between the top and the bottom. In Baldersdale we used cotton wool which made quilts difficult to wash but she said that with polyester you can machine wash very successfully providing you choose a very gentle cycle.

The 'batting' causes the puffed effect when sewed down with a quilting stitch using eight to ten stitches an inch. I think it was what I would call a running stitch with an occasional back stitch.

I learned a lot about the Amish way of life through a charming couple called Sterling and Robin Schoen, who run a boarding house in an old stone dwelling right in the middle of the most conservative community near Intercourse. Sterling had been a lawyer near Philadelphia, but tired of what he

Sterling and Robin Schoen outside their home.

A greeting from Oliver, the dog.

called the rat-race, and he and Robin were very happy catering for the constant flow of tourists attracted to Lancaster County by the Amish. They had a lovely, big black dog called Oliver, who sat and watched as we talked, sitting in rocking chairs in the shade of their garden. Sterling had made a study of the Amish, and said they originated from Switzerland in the sixteenth century and had been dreadfully persecuted until they came to America – although I was glad to hear that they were reasonably tolerated in England before departing for the New World. The community living around the Schoens stemmed from Germany, and still spoke a Rhine dialect. Indeed, the children did not begin to learn English until they started their education at the age of seven, and even then they went to one-room Amish schools. In that way they were isolated from outside influence. Then their education finished at the pre-high school stage, at what they call the eighth grade, and they went straight to work on the land. And from a very young age they were all allocated jobs to do in the home or on the farm, which gave them even less time to mix with non-Amish children and find out what the outside world was really

Typical Amish buggy.

40

like. Still, they did have an area of choice later on in life. You cannot be baptised into the Amish faith until you become a full adult, so the chance to opt out did occur but very few took the opportunity. After baptism, the rules were very strict in the more traditional groups. You cannot marry outside the faith, or fly in an aeroplane. Travel in a car was permitted, as long as you don't own or drive it, and trains and boats were also acceptable. You had to keep your feet on the ground, so to speak. Now those particular rules would suit me well, as it happens, but generally I am not a lover of restrictions, so I doubt I would make a good Amish despite my previous lifestyle.

Sterling said owning motorised transport was banned because the main aim was to keep the family together and cars would give youngsters a chance to travel and experience other ways. You could not go very far in a horse and buggy. He described how, if you broke the code badly, you were 'shunned'. No other Amish could speak to you or hand you anything, even your immediate family. I didn't like the thought of that – a horrid thing to do to your very own.

Cars proved to be a threat to the Amish in another way, because their buggies were constantly in danger on those narrow roads, when two or three motor vehicles bunched together in either direction and tried to overtake Amish families on the move. The two forms of transport were clearly incompatible – you cannot control a horse like you can a car. I saw several near misses, and then late one afternoon as they were returning in the crew vehicle to our hotel, Mostafa and Chris came across the aftermath of a very unpleasant accident. A blue car, seemingly driven by a girl who had two female companions, had collided with a horse pulling an Amish buggy as it attempted to pass. The car ended up in a ditch badly crumpled, and the poor horse had been injured, although it was still on its feet. An elderly Amish lady, clearly shocked, was complaining of an injury to her knee. An Amish gentleman of even more advanced years was explaining to a friend, partly in German I think, what had happened. It seems the brakes of the car may have failed.

Mostafa and Chris discreetly recorded what they could of the incident, but the camera was eventually spotted and they were told to 'get rid of that thing!' So they quietly departed – we had all agreed that great care must be taken to avoid offending the Amish.

A big team, still toiling at sunset.

Most of the Amish farms were rather small, around seventy or eighty acres, so working the land with horses did make economic sense, particularly when there were many willing hands and you didn't have to pay wages. Ecologically, it was very desirable, of course, and the land was some of the most fertile in America, which must prove something about the way they work it. But I noticed that some of them would make small concessions to ease the burden of life. We watched one family haymaking with a team of horses and a motor-driven baler mounted on the wagon. It was a strange sight, a curious combination of old and new. A little Ferguson tractor would have made the job so much easier. I also heard that some also used batteries to light their homes.

Sunday worship was held in one of their homes, and the location was known only to the Amish, week by week. By chance, we came across one such event being held at a large farm – it was easier to spot once you were passing by, because twenty or thirty buggies were parked about the farmyard. I noticed that they had managed to place several behind barns

Buggies parked outside in numbers indicates an Amish Sunday service.

and outbuildings as if to avoid attracting attention, but there were too many to hide them all away. Apparently the services start at 11 a.m. and last for three hours. Then they all had a meal. Afterwards the children were allowed to play in the fields whilst the adults sat in the sunshine and chatted. They were at that stage of the proceedings when we went by, and it did seem to be a happy, social occasion.

Another exceedingly odd thing about the Amish was the way they refer to everyone not of their faith. It didn't matter if you were American, European, Oriental, black, white, or whatever: you were 'English'. The habit is believed to reach back two centuries to when America was a British colony.

I went one day to a horse auction in New Holland which was fascinating. Outside they were selling everything from bales of hay to the most beautiful western-style saddles, and there were plenty of Amish about, bartering with each other and the 'English'. I was surprised when one or two of them came up and talked to me and even tolerated the camera for a while. They normally have a strong aversion to having their picture taken, so my camera crew always worked very discreetly to avoid causing offence. Then we discovered there was a curious way around this particular restriction. If you requested permission to film them they had to refuse, but if it was done from a distance and obviously not 'set up' then it seemed to be acceptable for a limited time. If one of their senior ministers chanced to see them on television, a very unlikely happening, they could genuinely say it was done without their agreement.

Incidentally, I was told they had elected bishops, but they were not distinguishable in any way by dress and remained full-time farmers.

One of the Amish who talked to me that day said that recently he had undergone a heart bypass operation, which cost 40,000 dollars. The surgeon's bill was paid in full by his brother Amish, who also gave him 5,000 dollars a month until he was fit to return to work. He described the Amish as one big family. He wanted to know what I was doing in New Holland and where I was from. When I told him that I came from Yorkshire he asked if that was anywhere near Germany, and whether I spoke German! So I explained that Yorkshire was part of Britain and that Germany was on the other side of the English Channel. And I was sorry, but I did not speak German.

Amish children at play.

New Holland is one of the larger towns in Amish country and must add to the confusion created by the popular description of the area as 'Pennsylvania Dutch country'. Even the local tourist bureau used the term in all its literature. But 'Dutch' is a corruption of 'Deutsch', or German, and it was certainly clear where the roots were of the gentleman who wondered if Yorkshire was a neighbour of Germany.

The clamour of the horse auction.

Inside the auction ring it was all noise and confusion, and I could hardly understand a word the auctioneer said. Our auctioneers can talk very quickly, but this was just a babble. And I was less than happy about the condition of some of the horses. I would guess they had not come from the best of homes, since some had marks on their backs and one I noticed had a cut down the leading side of its rear quarters. And I could have cried when I saw the matted coats on one or two of the younger horses. Nor did I care much for the way one Amish man used his whip. He was standing by the entrance to the ring and was obviously selling some of his own horses. One man rode them all into the ring, and he was a very skilled horseman because quite a few were rather frisky. I was told that the Amish rarely rode their horses, and they are not as sentimental about their animals as the British. Apparently, everyone has to pull their weight, people and beasts. Sterling Schoen said he knew one family who sold their dog because it didn't bark loudly enough when visitors came to their farm!

Now I must make it clear that I am not being critical of these simple country folk, because I appreciate and admire their principles, except the more extreme kind. There are several branches of their church, such as the Mennonites and the Brethren, and I met nothing but politeness and friendship on the occasions I had personal contact. They were jointly referred to as the Plain People and I certainly preferred the pace of their life, coming so soon after the hectic and headlong rush of New York. Even the local train service in Lancaster County is steam powered, but it would not exist but for tourism. I went on a ride to Strasburg and Paradise and back and enjoyed it very much. You really do enter a different age in Lancaster County.

Then I was granted a rare privilege on my last day. I was invited by the Meyer family to go for a buggy ride and then join them for dinner. I sat beside Mr Jack Meyer, a large, bearded man dressed in the traditional manner, and as we drove through the rolling countryside we spoke farmer to farmer, about crops and the various breeds of animals and the fields in view. He had a grand horse, a very comfortable buggy and a great sense of humour.

The train to Paradise!

Mr Meyer said he had worked with horses all his life, and his earliest memory went back to the time when he was two and half years old, pleading with his grandfather to let him take the reins of a horse! The request was, understandably, refused.

He was a mine of information about the area, saying that there were around four thousand, eight hundred Amish farms in Lancaster County alone. They were almost exclusively dairy farms, milking over ninety thousand head and growing corn and hay to feed them. I said that I had noticed that the land seemed very fertile, and he told me that it was red clay and limestone. When the early settlers came from the Rhine Valley they recognised its value and staked their claims.

I wasn't surprised to hear that the Amish farmers were early risers, because milking twice a day, three hundred and sixty five days a year – there is no escape – is probably the most demanding way to farm. Certainly without the benefit of electricity, and I can speak from experience because I kept a milk cow or two in the past. The standard Amish day starts at 4.30 a.m., and the milking goes on until breakfast at seven.

Buggy ride with Jack Meyer.

Half an hour later the children are packed off to school, which starts at eight, and then the men start work with the horses until lunch is served by their ladies at eleven. The horses are usually put away around three in the afternoon and then the final milking of the day begins. That is followed by supper, and by seven thirty most farmers are in bed. A tough regime, maybe, but I can vouch that there are compensations – and they won't need sleeping pills!

I assumed since the land was so good that very few beef cattle would be kept, but Mr Meyer said that, on the contrary, many thousands were reared in the region but they were habitually kept in the barns – 'to prevent them running around and losing weight'!

However, I think my assumption was correct, because he went on to say that with the combination of rich soil and favourable climate – the place was close enough to the sea to benefit from regular moisture – it was possible to plant corn after the wheat harvest. To a Northern hill farmer that was pretty remarkable. Apparently, the growing season was so

'Is Yorkshire near Germany!' – conversation with an Amish gentleman outside the horse auction.

Amish produce on the way to market.

long that you could plant corn at any time from the middle of May to the middle of July and still be assured of a crop.

As we drove along, he pointed out a team of six mules hauling a machine which was breaking up the ground so that corn could be planted. We paused to watch, and when I told him that I had only heard of mules before arriving in Lancaster County, he asked pointedly if I had ever heard anything good about them! He obviously preferred Shire horses for that kind of work, since he owned two of those magnificent animals himself and was a life member of the American Shire Horse Association.

Mr Meyer's good humour bubbled to the surface again when we passed a long line of washing and he described it as the Amish version of a solar-powered drying machine! Then we came across a one-room Amish school with two outside toilets, one for the girls and one for the boys, and I was able to tell him that I attended a similar school in Baldersdale.

Dinner with the Meyers was a remarkable experience. They do take in paying guests, but you are not to use alcohol prior to

Dee Dee Meyer preparing a dessert.
. . . and slicing home made bread.
Rachel Meyer slicing carrots.
Miriam Meyer with flowers for the table and right, Dee Dee, Judy (family friend) and Rachel prepare the table.

your arrival, and not to smoke on their property. Most importantly, you were specifically requested not to bring a camera with you.

But . . . for my benefit, they allowed us to film them at their table with no restrictions. It was a rare honour and I do hope the Meyers won't get into trouble with their bishops as a consequence.

The goodness of the Meyers shone from them. They were members of the River Brethren, a much more relaxed group, but when they had built their large wooden house, the friendship and co-operation between the various branches was made very evident. It was largely self-constructed, with Amish, Mennonite and Brethren working shoulder to shoulder. If you need help in these parts, everyone comes to do their bit just like the old days in Baldersdale. Countryfolk must be the same all around the world.

A big home it was, too, but necessarily so, since Jack and Dee Dee Meyer have six children, all with lovely biblical sounding names – Jessica, Joshua, Sarah, Rachel, Miriam and Caleb. And do they eat!

Mr Meyer began by saying Grace in such a simple and moving way – I'm sure it was totally spontaneous:

Kindly, Gracious, Heavenly Father, we thank you for your great mercy and graciousness, and the gift of another day so we can serve you. We thank you for this food and the house that we share. We thank you for our lovely guest, and for my wife who has laboured so carefully and lovingly to prepare this meal. I pray for your blessing on each and every one, and for all these things we give praise and thanks to Jesus Christ. Amen.

Lancaster Amish are famous for their food, and justifiably so. I suppose they need a lot of nourishment to enable them to work such long and strenuous hours, and the ladies go to a lot of trouble to make it tasty. Mrs Meyer placed a huge bowl of chicken barley soup before her husband, who served it out, informing us as he did so that if you asked an Amish family what they were having for supper they would traditionally say: 'Oh, just soup and bread.'

I would call that a traditional Amish joke, because I lost count of the number of courses I was offered that night. Most I had never heard of before, but they were delicious, every one. Mr Meyer said it was usual to serve guests seven sweets and

Dinner with the Meyer family.

seven sours. The sours were the pickles, and I was urged to try Mrs Meyer's pickled beets which he said were the best in the world. Fortunately I am fond of pickled food and enjoyed everything on offer, including something called chow chow which turned out to be pickled mixed vegetables. The region is also celebrated for its meat loaves, and one of the main courses was a ham loaf with no ham! It was made from beef and smoked turkey, but it was customary, for obscure reasons, to label it 'ham'.

Then came the seven sweets. Mrs Meyer had won prizes for her desserts, and I was quite overwhelmed. Deep pineapple pudding, chocolate coconut pie, chocolate rolls covered in powdered sugar called Eskimos, flans, and one called Shoo-Fly pie. Apparently, in the past when the Amish put fruit pies outside to cool, they would place a sticky, sweet concoction topped generously with molasses nearby to divert the flies. This throwaway dish had subsequently been developed into a status dessert, and Mrs Meyer had perfected it!

Jugs of iced water washed down this feast, but midway through we were offered tea. Meadow tea. It was made from herbs which grow wild. I was told they could be found under the pretty covered bridge (no one could explain why some required roofing) which we could see from the window of the dining room. The herbs were placed, green and fresh, straight into the pot and usually flavoured with mint or lemon. It was the Meyer's staple beverage, taken with all meals and last thing at night. During the summer they would drink it iced from the fridge. They were clearly anxious to know my opinion – my goodness, I did experience some remarkable varieties of tea during my tour of America – and after a period of uncertainty, I must confess that I found it very nice and refreshing.

When the meal was finished, the children were allowed to play out in the large garden – one of the girls galloped a horse down the lane – whilst we talked over the meadow tea. I asked Mr Meyer to explain the differences between the various religious orders in Lancaster County. He said there were three groups of what he called 'Plain People': the Amish, the Mennonites and the Brethren. But they in turn had split into many groups – there were four kinds of Brethren, and as many as twenty of the Mennonites. One sect of the latter were the most strict and conservative of them all. Whilst most of the Amish used gas-powered cookers and fridges during the heat and humidity of the summer, when temperatures could reach one hundred fahrenheit (they switched to wood-burning stoves in the winter), some Mennonites would not even have indoor plumbing, never mind electricity or gas. Nor would they travel in a car like the rest, who would hire a car with a driver to maintain their distance from motorised transport.

But Mr Meyer's group allowed electricity, although he only worked his land with horses. He said he had once discussed his way of life with an Amish minister and asked respectfully for his opinion. The reply was: 'What do I think? Why, you are as Amish as I am!'

Apparently, as far as theology is concerned all the groups are similar. There was no resentment shown to those who opted for modern comforts.

Judy picking mint for the tea.

There was clearly a lot of love and laughter in the Meyer household, and the children were exceedingly well behaved. They all returned obediently to the dining room when the final ritual of the evening was to begin. They formed a group with their mother and father and sang a hymn in a manner I had not heard before, all harmonising beautifully.

All in all, a vivid and memorable occasion. I felt very proud, humble even, to be received in this way. Politicians have talked a lot recently about family values, including ex-president George Bush when he was campaigning in vain to return to the White House. They would all, perhaps, be well advised to examine the ways and habits of the gentlefolk of Lancaster County if they wish to know the true meaning of family unity.

4

Tea and Sympathy at Gettysburg

I know for certain that the Amish would refuse to be involved in any way with the event that made the otherwise insignificant town of Gettysburg a permanent feature in the history books. Fighting, or violence of any kind, was absolutely out of the question for the Amish, and on the attractive wooded hills around Gettysburg there were three dreadful days in the month of July 1863, which shaped the future of America. It was a very close run thing, as Wellington said after Waterloo, but the North finally won the decisive battle against the South. General Robert E. Lee, commander of the Confederate armies, surrendered shortly after his troops were forced to flee from Gettysburg.

The entire battleground is now a national monument dotted with memorials, statues, cannons and other solemn reminders of the fighting. There were more than fifty thousand casualties of one sort or another: killed, wounded or missing in action. And it provoked a strange feeling in me, to be standing in the middle of a place which had seen so much pain and suffering. It was not a spot I would choose to visit – indeed, it was the first battlefield I had ever seen – but I can understand people's interest due to the historical importance. I was there simply because of the television programme's requirements.

I understand that Gettysburg and other unfortunate scenes of bloodshed became tourist attractions very soon after the American Civil War, even for the British. The Thomas Cook Company certainly arranged excursions for their clients as the

The High Water Mark at Gettysburg.

COMMANDS HONORED.

railroads were built across America, and I believe they even witnessed the final clearing away of some of the wreckage of war. That was one Cook's tour I would have declined.

I do, however, understand the need to pay homage, and the memorials and monuments were quite splendid; but I felt a chill in my spine, particularly at the place they call the 'High Watermark' of the Confederate's struggle to win the war. On the third day, General Lee threw twelve thousand men at the Union lines, which was described as his last desperate gamble. They did manage to break through briefly, but the Southern forces had lost so many men through artillery and rifle fire on the way across open country that they finally succumbed to the sheer weight of numbers. I understand that the slaughter on both sides in those few hours was fearful, and they placed the 'High Watermark' monument on the very spot where the tide finally turned against the South.

Altogether 160,000 men were involved, and when the two exhausted armies moved on they left six thousand, dead and dying, just lying on the field of battle – more than the living population of Gettysburg at the time. Volunteers hastily buried the dead, since the weather was very hot, and cared for the wounded, but it was apparently very slapdash and in later months farmers ploughing the fields for planting began to turn up bodies. A hateful thought.

Eventually, a proper cemetery was created and Abraham Lincoln, the North's leader and then president of the entire country, came in November of the same year to dedicate it. Lincoln only spoke for two minutes, but his words became immortal, ending with the famous phrase:

. . . That we here highly resolve that these dead shall not have died in vain – that this nation, under God, shall have a new birth of freedom – and that government of the people, by the people, for the people, shall not perish from the earth.

Just a few of the battlefield memorials.

I have to confess I was a trifle hazy about the reasons for the American Civil War, but I was reminded that the basic problem was the South's reluctance to end slavery, so the cause was a good one. Still, it's a pity it had to be resolved in this manner. And I understand that some families were divided, with brother fighting against brother, which must have been a nightmare for their parents. I went to visit the cemetery, and I came across row upon row of tiny, numbered headstones; just

white cubes stretching away into the distance. A nearby inscription read: '425 bodies, Unknown'. What a way to end your life – no name, just a number.

The full story of the Gettysburg battle is told continuously to tourists in a remarkable round building which houses something they call the Cyclorama, a panoramic painting 26 feet high and 365 feet in length, done by a French artist in 1884. It depicts in vivid detail that last Southern attack on the Union lines known as Picket's Charge, and you stand on a platform completely surrounded by scenes of carnage and horror. A soundtrack is played of cannon and rifle fire and the shouts and screams of men doing their best to kill each other. It was so loud you really felt you were in the middle of the battle and I had to cover my ears at one stage. I became very confused by the commentary, which was rather rapid, and I had to keep swivelling round as they picked out various points of interest by using lights. It would have been better for me had it been on one screen in front of me, like the cinema. I didn't know for sure which side was which most of the time, but the show was very effective and obviously had educational value for history students.

For me, there was one other memorable occasion during my visit to Gettysburg. It may sound trivial when set against the momentous happenings in that place, but it occurred at the place where we lodged for the night. It had taken us some time to find it when we arrived in Gettysburg, because Thomas Cook usually book us into very large and easily located hotels. But the Brafferton Inn was quite tiny, dating back to the eighteenth century – which meant it was there during the fighting – and only had ten rooms. But I felt more at home and comfortable there than in far grander places. First of all, my room was on the ground floor so I had no lifts (or elevators, as they are called in America) to negotiate – I'm still not trained to use them unescorted. And it was run by the most charming couple, Sam and Jane Back, who took a keen interest in me. Nothing was too much trouble for them.

And then the great event occurred. I ordered tea, which I always do on arrival somewhere, and sat back expecting the usual do-it-yourself jug of lukewarm water and a tea-bag. Mrs Back appeared with a proper teapot, and a real English brew already mashing away.

It was the first time that had happened since before we had arrived in New York.

Mrs Back and her teapot at the Brafferton Inn.

44

5

Washington and My Visit to the White House

Now, I liked Washington a lot. It reminded me of Paris, with all those marvellous buildings and plenty of trees; and the streets were even wider than the French capital, which surprised me.

The drive there from Gettysburg was quite an experience. I've become accustomed in the last two or three years to British motorways, but the freeway to Washington was different – ten lanes of traffic, five going in each direction and all full most of the time. Sometimes when you crested a rise you could see ahead a mile or more. There must have been thousands of cars in view, rushing along either with you, or towards you. It was quite alarming.

We had previously encountered a few problems entering American cities in search of a place to rest our weary heads, because the road systems and signposting were very strange, even to experienced British drivers. When we drove from Philadelphia to Lancaster County to meet the Amish, just one wrong decision had led us almost half way back to New York, and we had real difficulty trying to weave our way towards the right direction. Thus, a one-and-a-half hour journey turned into something over four hours.

But we entered the downtown area of Washington without a hitch and at one stage, according to the map, we were within half a mile of our hotel, which was located on E Street Northwest. Naturally, we assumed E was short for East, but when we stopped to ask a local for directions he said he had

Washington, DC, with the Capitol in the background.

never heard of East Street. Sure enough – there was no East Street. Most American cities give numbers to their streets, such as First Street, Second Street, Fifth Avenue and so, but in Washington they also give them letters so you have A, B, C Street etc. Realisation dawned after a few more enquiries, and within ten minutes we were checking into our hotel. It turned out, in one way, to be a home from home for me.

It was called the Belle Vue, which is the name of my cottage back in Cotherstone, and a likeable, eccentric place it was. The lifts were very old and operated by attendants which suited me down to the ground (literally, you could say), but it was a first class hotel everywhere, with the friendliest of staff. They had a bar designed to resemble a British pub which even served yards of ale. The ladies were offered a more decorous half-yard, and the novelty went down very well with the customers.

Our stay in the capital city of America was mainly a happy and sunlit occasion with the possible exception of our first

Home from home – the Belle Vue Hotel.

A black place – the Vietnam Memorial.

assignment for the television series, which was to visit the Vietnam War Memorial. Gettysburg was hard enough to bear, but this was an infinitely more painful place. Vietnam was so recent by comparison, and the memorial – a sombre, black marble wall carved with the names of all those who had died in the war – was crowded with people, and some were visibly affected. I would imagine that they were there to see the names of people close to them, husbands or fathers perhaps. Bunches of flowers and letters and poems, some obviously written by children, were placed all around the base, and some single roses, which I thought most poignant. I felt somehow that I shouldn't have been there, in the middle of such private grief. Barry Cockcroft met and spoke to men in uniform who had served in Vietnam, there to read the names and pay tribute to friends and comrades who had fallen alongside them. One in particular was so affected that he was unable to speak.

Just over 58,000 American soldiers died or went missing over the long years of that particular war, which was another battle between North and South with the North winning, just like the American Civil War. Only that time, it was the wrong side as far as the Americans were concerned. It was all in vain. I thought of the Gettysburg men and their three days of horror, but they didn't have the benefit of proper medical aid or helicopters to carry them to field hospitals. How many would have survived if they had? War is just a terrible tragedy – any war.

A short while after my visit, President Bill Clinton came to the Vietnam memorial to kneel at the spot where the name of one of his classmates who'd been killed in action was inscribed, and he made a rubbed impression to take away – I saw several people doing that myself. The occasion was Memorial Day, a national holiday when it is the custom to honour the warriors who fell fighting for America. I'm afraid the new president had a mixed reception from the crowd, because he managed to avoid serving in Vietnam himself and had opposed the war.

Close by that black place, there is a happier memorial to someone I particularly admire. A man who made it from log cabin to White House, Abraham Lincoln. It was an awe inspiring building, quite enormous, with a giant statue of him sitting on a chair. He looks out towards the Washington Memorial, a high stone column that reflects in a rectangular pool of water between the two structures. It occurred to me whilst I was walking around the Lincoln statue that America seems to kill off its best men – the Kennedy brothers and Martin Luther King, for instance, felled by assassin's bullets in their prime, just like Lincoln.

A visit to the White House was high on my Washington agenda and it was a thrill to see it for the first time, although I had imagined it bigger than it actually was. In Britain, we have lots of private country houses which are much more imposing. But one has to be impressed since it is the home of the most

The Lincoln Memorial.

In the background, the Washington Memorial.

powerful man in the world (although that could be a matter of opinion in some quarters). I was asked which I admired most of the presidents who had lived there in my lifetime, and I had to start with Franklin D. Roosevelt, who was such a help to Britain during the Second World War. He and Winston Churchill were good friends as well as military allies. Then there was Eisenhower and John F. Kennedy, but I am going to put at the top of my personal list the man who walked to the White House on his own two feet, without any pomp or ceremony: Jimmy Carter. It's the man that counts when all's said and done, and although he may have been lacking experience, I am sorry he did not get a second chance at office. He had to handle the hostage crisis, which was the first of its kind to confront an American leader. There were plenty more after he left, so I consider fate was rather unkind to Jimmy Carter. I liked his simplicity, and I suppose the fact that he was a farmer like me had something to do with it too. As it happens he had agreed to meet me, after Barry Cockcroft had written to his office in Georgia saying that I was to visit America and would dearly love the honour of shaking his hand. His secretary named two dates but – alas! – I was on the QE2 in the middle of the North Atlantic on both the days in question. She tried hard to find an alternative but there was not another moment available in his diary during my entire stay, which demonstrated how busy and important he still was. Apparently our visit coincided with a touring schedule he had arranged across the United States. It was a real disappointment for me.

We had also asked if we could meet someone from the President Clinton household, maybe even the man himself, but in the end they wouldn't allow our cameras nearer than the railings around the White House. Indeed, we were informed that even the simplest still camera was not admitted for security reasons. I could understand that, really, because any

The White House.

president of the United States seems a permanent target for madmen. Even President Reagan was shot down.

But they did let me in. Not that it was any great achievement, because all you have to do is queue at a nearby kiosk early in the morning and anyone will be given a free ticket to join a tour of the White House on a first come, first served basis. It was a very efficient operation. The ticket specified a certain time and we were swiftly marshalled into a slow-moving crocodile, through the security screening where my handbag was X-rayed. I noticed the route for you to follow was watched over every inch of the way by guards. One even pounced on Barry Cockcroft, who was escorting me, because he thought Barry's tape recorder was a camera.

There was a curious but amusing incident when our tickets were torn as we entered the garden of the White House. The security man asked if I was from Britain, and when I told him I was he asked if I had any matches on my person. I assured him that I hadn't, and wondered for a moment if I would be searched. Then he laughed and said the British had burned down the White House in 1814, and he wouldn't want it to happen again. I was next to a large and boisterous group of schoolchildren from Birmingham, Alabama, at the time and they thought it all very funny.

I changed my first impression of the White House when I saw the inside of it. I thought it combined grandeur and comfort, really unusual and very pleasant. There were huge bowls of fresh flowers everywhere, and the rooms were generally smaller than you would expect, which gave the place a more lived-in feeling than, say, Buckingham Palace. Even the State Dining Room was modest in size, but the notice said it would seat 140 people. I couldn't imagine how. We progressed through the East Room, the Green Room and the Red Room, which apparently is often used by the First Lady to receive guests, and the Blue Room, which had lovely varnished woodwork and was oval in shape. But we didn't get a glimpse of that other oval room where the president has his office, nor see anything of the Clintons, although I did talk to a gentleman and his young daughter in the queue who had actually spoken to President Clinton that very morning. Apparently, he makes a habit of jogging around the public lawns near the White House, and he had stopped when he saw the little girl and said how much he liked her sweater, which was very colourful. She was obviously thrilled to bits. Running around in public seems

The grave of John F. Kennedy.

rather dangerous to me when you consider the past, but the girl's father told me he was surrounded by security men.

The portraits on the walls of the White House turned out to be the most interesting part of the visit. They really brought the romance and drama of the recent past home to you, and there was a bit of controversy involved as well. Apparently, it was customary to display the portraits of the last seven presidents to the public gaze, but President Clinton had broken with tradition. He ordered those of Presidents Nixon and Reagan removed, and they were replaced by Franklin D. Roosevelt and Harry Truman. I consider he had the right to do so seeing as it is his house, at least for the time being, and if he liked them, then why not? I dearly liked the portrait of Roosevelt, because in profile he looked so much like Lord Louis Mountbatten. They were both very handsome men in my opinion. I spotted the portrait of President Reagan tucked quite a distance away up a staircase, but President Nixon's had disappeared altogether. At the start of our tour there was a painting of Mrs Nancy Reagan prominently displayed, looking like a rake dressed up, she was so thin. I'm afraid I didn't think much of President Reagan and his policies, which were close to those of Mrs Thatcher. They may have been good for certain sections of the community, but not so good for others. I was never sure where President Reagan's acting ended and his real life began. Maybe he was a good man in his way, but not a president I could admire.

There was a very strange portrait displayed of President Kennedy, with his head bowed so you couldn't see his face. I was told that the artist never met his subject and wouldn't do the face and perhaps portray a false expression, which was wise. Altogether a sad painting, which was very apt when you consider what happened to the man.

On our last day in Washington we went to see where President Kennedy was buried. Arlington Cemetery is calculated to send a chill down the spine of anyone, since it is mainly a military cemetery and there are hundreds of acres of little white headstones stretching as far as the eye can see. I believe it was opened after the American Civil War and the thousands who fell in that unfortunate conflict are buried there, together with those who died fighting for the American flag in subsequent wars. The tomb of the Unknown Warrior is also placed there and I watched as they changed the guard mounted alongside it, with much ceremony. Everything is so neat and beautifully kept, with shaved lawns and lots of trees.

But the John Fitzgerald Kennedy grave was the most moving part of our visit to Arlington Cemetery. I was aware that he inspired an entire generation, and at least one of our party was clearly affected. Before we left, Barry Cockcroft asked me to read out loud the final part of his historic inaugration speech, carved in stone next to the eternal flame over his grave, and concluding with the words that rang around the world.

'And so my fellow Americans,
ask not what your country can do for you,
ask what you can do for your country.
My fellow citizens of the world, ask not what
America will do for you, but what together
we can do for the freedom of Man.'

. . . and the words that rang round the world.

6

Back to the Colonial Past in Virginia

By the time I reached the lush pastures of Virginia, apparently one of the wealthiest states in America, I concluded that the people of the United States regarded their history with a particular reverence. Perhaps it's because they have so little of it when compared to Britain, they have a need to extract every ounce of value and interest out of their past. Everywhere we went, from Philadelphia onwards, we were handed large quantities of literature which was backed up by personal explanations of the historical development of whichever area we were visiting at the time. They were so knowledgeable and so proud of their heritage, however limited, and I had to reflect how little I could have told them about the history of England – even that which concerns the place where I live. For instance, I would have been quite unable to paint any real picture of our civil war. I know Cromwell and his roundheads were fighting the king and his cavaliers and the Yorkshire Dales saw some action, but that's about it. Indeed, I am now better acquainted with the facts of the American Civil War after visiting Gettysburg and Virginia. Most of the big battles before Gettysburg seem to have taken place in the Richmond area, and there were reminders and memorials for each and every one. And the Americans have recently developed and just about perfected a way of recreating the past in a very effective and dramatic manner.

'Living History' they call it, and the most outstanding example I found was in Williamsburg, Virginia. Thankfully, it

A covered wagon in Williamsburg – with the old British flag.

was not dominated by the Civil War, but based entirely on the early settlers from Britain who founded Williamsburg in the seventeenth century, and made it into a major political and cultural centre of America. It was a startling experience to walk into the centre of Williamsburg – like journeying back into the past. Everything is as it was in the seventeenth and eighteenth centuries. Even the people who live there dress as their forebears did. All the shops and taverns are genuine period buildings which have been recreated with great care and much expense, and the only transport allowed is horse-powered in the strict sense of the word. Eighty eight of the buildings there are the original colonial structures, and the rest have been built as accurately as possible on the original foundations, so the entire town looks very much like it was two centuries ago. They call it a museum, but it is very different to any museum I have ever seen. They even researched the type and number of trees growing in the town in the old days and planted exactly the same. There is no trace of the twentieth century, apart from the tourists.

The main street, named after the Duke of Gloucester to keep the British sovereign happy, since the Duke was the heir apparent, is about a mile long and lined mostly with white framed colonial buildings and the occasional brick structure. There is nothing built from stone, because they had no access to quarries at the time. Probably the best and most picturesque of them is the Governor's palace, which later became the capitol, and was last occupied by Thomas Jefferson before he was elected Governor of the Commonwealth. There was also a courthouse built in 1770 and a parish church which was completed the same year that Christopher Wren finished St Paul's cathedral in London.

Despite its importance, the number of people resident in Williamsburg before Independence was only eighteen hundred, yet the population of Virginia was half a million at the time. Since life was almost exclusively based on agriculture, the great majority of people lived on outlying farms.

From the very start, everything in Williamsburg was modelled on the British way of life, both politically and socially, since it was part of the British Empire and allegiance was shown to the Crown. Even today, they fly the old British flag over the capitol, similar to the Union Jack but without the cross of St Patrick, which is historically correct. It must have been a real achievement to establish a true British culture in a place where fifty years before there had only been a forest inhabited by Indians. Fashions and manners were derived from whatever intelligence arrived on the ships from home, and elections were held in the British manner, with a vote only being given to those who owned property. However, as nearly everyone had land – there was so much of it – I was told that there were proportionately more people with the vote in Virginia than anywhere else in the world. Things were rather different after the revolution and the Declaration of Independence, which was signed by at least one descendant of a Williamsburg family. They changed the name of the King's Arms tavern to The Eagle and even had their own Liberty Bell which is still in good shape, unlike the cracked one in Philadelphia.

A ride round Colonial Williamsburg.

I was given a ride in a horse and carriage around Williamsburg with a guide, and later introduced to some of the

residents who portray actual people who lived there in colonial times. They are actors and actresses really, and the place is just a stage for them. They do occupy the houses on a full time, paid, basis. It's all run on National Trust lines, I suppose, and visitors come in droves from all around the world to experience Williamsburg – and an experience it truly is.

My first call was at the Apothecary. The lady in charge offered me some of the remedies available two hundred years ago, some of which are still on sale in various forms in chemist's shops today. Oil of turpentine for instance, which is still rubbed into aching muscles, and camphorated oil to apply to the chest, clearing sinuses and helping you breathe when you have a cold or bronchitis. She could also offer a mixture of ground chalk and oyster shells, a splendid source of calcium to cure indigestion and dyspepsia, and the bark of a tree from the Caribbean from which you could extract quinine to alleviate fevers such as malaria. They were all contained in the original jars and decorated tins. Personally, I believe in the old remedies and still use some that my grandmother gave to me as a child, such as wintergreen, knitbone and aconite; and I understand that modern medicine is looking very seriously into claims that at least some of the answers to problematic diseases can be found in nature's garden, particularly from plants growing in the forests of South America.

But there was one treatment available at the apothecary's establishment which certainly did not appeal to me. In the eighteenth century, doctors were still working out the mysteries of circulation, and believed that sometimes it could flow too quickly causing heat and friction. For this, they prescribed blood letting – by attaching leeches to the body to suck the blood out. The thought of this made me cringe and – would you believe – the lady produced a real live leech from a box under the counter. You may say that was carrying authenticity a little too far. But to please her I had a look at it, at the same time remarking that the cure may be worse than the ailment. Leeches were also used to reduce swellings and bruises and they were allowed to stay attached until they became bloated. It was scant comfort to be told that they only drank around two spoonfuls – but she didn't say how big a spoon she meant!

Then I was taken to meet the Merry Widow of Williamsburg, an amazing lady playing the part of the wife of the late Peyton Randolph, a man who held high office in the colony for many

A visit to the Apothecary.

years until his death in 1737. Dressed in the most splendid mourning apparel of the time, she granted me an audience in the very house she and her 'late husband' had occupied, which was naturally one of the finest in the town. After admiring my hat and saying how nice it was to welcome a personage from the mother country she then unleashed a torrent of conversation and information using the polite language and mannerisms of the society lady she was representing. She got under the skin of Mrs Randolph so skilfully that it was almost like being transported back in time to the eighteenth century. Indeed, she treated me as though I was a visitor from that time,

In conversation with the 'Merry Widow'.

referring delicately to the 'unpleasantness taking place betwixt the mother country and her fair colony – in plain language, the struggle by America to win her independence – and saying that ladies must not discuss matters of government. It was much better to talk of the latest fashions, and of forthcoming balls and assemblies. She was anxious to know if I considered the people of Williamsburg 'civilised', because she understood that there was an opinion currently held in London that it was a wild place, and because of that the wives of some governors appointed by the crown did not wish to accompany their husbands when they came to take up their duties. She was delighted when I said that they had formed entirely the wrong impression and asked me to be an ambassador for Williamsburg upon my return home! It was, she declared, the most British of all the colonies, having been founded at the start of the sixteenth century. The early settlers found that wearing armour was very uncomfortable in the heat of the Virginia summer, but was considered necessary because of the danger from 'savages lurking behind every bush'.

Bidding farewell outside her splendid residence.

I asked if they had any trouble from the Indians these days – I meant, of course, the mid-eighteenth century – and she told me that relations had improved to such an extent that Indian boys were studying at the local college. But there were complaints from the elders of the tribe that their sons were returning with 'soft bellies and a disinclination to hunt'. Nevertheless, there was a growing opinion among the senior politicians of Williamsburg that some of the tribal chiefs display remarkable leadership qualities for savages and govern their people very well, indeed.

It was a marvellous performance from the lady, who was called Mary Wiseman, and I wasn't surprised to learn later that she was an actress of some note. It was quite an exhausting experience, too, for both of us – she scarcely drew breath for nearly twenty minutes and I found it difficult to get a word in edgeways.

Later on, I was relieved to be able to relax over a cup of tea in one of the taverns which specialised in live music. A very droll gentleman called John Turner played the fiddle to the assembled company, and he turned out to be a native of Argyllshire in Scotland, although he was now a naturalised American. He had left his homeland twenty-five years ago, and as well as being a very accomplished musician was also a Doctor of Theology and a member of the Presbyterian church. Finally, I was introduced to another figure from the past, an enormous coloured gentleman who was playing the part of a freed slave. Apparently, fifty per cent of the population of Williamsburg was of African descent, some free but most slaves. A rigid class system was obviously established immediately by the early settlers, run on British lines. You might imagine that starting from scratch in a virtual wilderness would have created a different sort of society, but when it finally became a proper community they displayed all the inequalities of the life they had fled. Two per cent of the population owned fifty per cent of the land, property, livestock and slaves.

I had a long conversation with the 'freed slave', a Mr Art Johnson, who had a drum which he used to illustrate the importance of music to the slaves. It was central to their lives. They used the rhythms to pace their work, following a caller who would lead the singing. He said it helped to take their minds off their misery. It was a culture they had brought with them all the way from Africa and it later spread to other

Tea and a little music.

sections of the community – for instance, the marching songs of the American military were said to stem from the negro working chants.

There were two basic kinds of slave, those who worked in the home and those who laboured in the fields. Most people believed that the domestic slaves had the best time of it, but the outdoor slaves could at least go home at the end of the day, whilst the domestics were at the beck and call of their master twenty-four hours a day. Everything hinged on the character and the moods of the master. In the home, slaves had to contend not only with their owner, but the owner's wife, his children and even his guests. Out in the fields they just had the overseer to worry about, and they did have the benefit of fresh air. And it wouldn't be possible to beat them all every day because there were too many of them.

Taking my ease in Colonial Williamsburg (*above*).

On a brighter note, it seems they were kinder to their slaves in Virginia than in some of the other Southern States. To begin with they grew tobacco, which was much less labour-intensive than cotton, so they did not need so many slaves.

Some were even given land to raise their own crops and animals, which they were allowed to sell in the market place to improve their standard of living.

However, I did notice on my tour of the United States that equality in the real sense was certainly not in place. Most of the low-paid jobs – the waiters, the porters, the cleaners – were invariably undertaken by coloured folk. You rarely saw a black face sitting in the best restaurants, or checking into the high class hotels.

My meeting with the 'Freed Slave' (*left*).

There's a way to go yet, and it saddened me.

7

Berkeley Plantation – and the Son of the Drummer Boy

America is a huge country and peopled with extraordinary personalities, but nowhere did I meet anyone with a more fascinating story to tell than that of Malcolm Jamieson, the master of the Berkeley Plantation in the agricultural heartland of Virginia.

The lovely, fertile acres of Berkeley had been mute witness to some of the most important developments in the early development of America, some inspirational and some violent. It was at Berkeley that the Union army established their camp after being beaten back in their attempt to capture Richmond, capital of the Confederacy. There they waited for Abraham Lincoln to send supplies and reinforcements via the sea to the James River which laps the estate. For two months, nearly one hundred and fifty thousand soldiers crowded the thousand acres of Berkeley, among them a twelve-year-old drummer boy from Scotland.

His name was John Jamieson . . . the father, no less, of Malcolm Jamieson!

I spent a pleasant, sunlit day at Berkeley with Malcolm Jamieson, who is a very active eighty-four-year-old, and he told me about the extraordinary sequence of events which led to the son of the little drummer boy becoming the owner of what is considered to be one of the finest plantations in all Virginia, which is adorned with many similar estates. Berkeley has been distinguished as a registered National Landmark. After a tour in an electrically-driven golf cart of his magnificent grounds,

Malcolm Jamieson tells me his story.

which include one of the best boxwood gardens in America, Mr Jamieson and I sat in the shade – very necessary, as the temperature soared up to the high eighties – and he told me his story.

His father sailed with his elder brother, Walter, from Scotland, and arrived in New York at a time when the Civil War had already started. They were given a home and cared for by another Scotsman, and were consequently very grateful to him. Only ten days after their arrival, their host was drafted into the Union army. Apparently, you were forced to go and fight unless you could pay three hundred dollars or find someone acceptable to go in your place. The man's wife and children were so upset at the prospect of losing him, and they didn't have the money being poor immigrants. So Malcolm's Uncle Walter volunteered to go in his place, telling his young brother to inform their mother that he had gone to war but wasn't quite sure which side he was on!

Walter Jamieson went on to become a legendary war hero, decorated with the highest honours for repeated acts of bravery. According to his nephew, the man was reckless in the extreme, always leading charges and sometimes going out alone and under heavy fire to drag wounded soldiers to safety. Nothing could harm him, it seemed. Men alongside him were being shot dead or blown apart, but he came through relatively unscathed. But Malcolm said that Uncle Walter went to pieces when the war ended. He began drinking bourbon whiskey and running around with an opera singer. In the end, the whiskey did what the bullets and shells failed to do. Such a shame – he deserved something better. In the meantime, the drummer boy, who had not been allowed to fight because of his youth, had been busy creating a very successful construction business in New York, building warehouses and docks, and even laid the base for the Statue of Liberty. He always remembered his time at Berkeley, and one day he decided he would have to start growing his own timber to make wooden piles for the dockwork in Manhattan. So he looked around for suitable land to buy and heard that Berkeley was for sale. It became his in 1907, more than forty years after he had spent time there under canvas. A year later Malcolm was born, and he started to help run the place at roughly the same age that his father had been when he first saw Berkeley. He nursed an ambition to be a farmer which apparently disappointed his father, who wanted him to become a harbour pilot in New York.

Aerial view of the Berkeley estate.

Malcolm said that he took over a virtual ruin. For years after the end of the war it had been sorely neglected. The Union army had chopped down all the trees for fuel, except for one clump to give shade to their cooks and their ovens, and left it a sea of mud. This puzzled me at first because I had noticed that the Berkeley Plantation of today was blessed with hundreds of mature trees, some very tall; then I recalled just how old Mr Malcolm Jamieson was. It was he who had planted them – and that was seventy years ago!

Over the decades, he and his wife Grace (her family fought for the South!) had restored both the house and the grounds. They still have hand-carved Adam woodwork that was first installed in the house in 1770, and Chippendale furniture and many other fine pieces. Their son, Malcolm Junior, and his wife

and their two children are all involved at Berkeley, so continuity seems assured. It remains very much a working plantation with five hundred acres planted with soya beans and grain crops, not tobacco.

The place had enjoyed a truly illustrious past before it was ravaged by war. It was one of the first great estates in the New World, and was home to the Harrison family from which sprang two presidents, two Governors and a signer of the Declaration of Independence.

A band of Gloucestershire men, only thirty-eight in number, first stepped on this land from their small boat moored in the James river on 4 December 1619, after a perilous voyage of three months which some of the original party did not survive. They knelt to give thanks as soon as they touched land, and this must have been the first official Thanksgiving in America, since they arrived more than a year before the pilgrim fathers sailed to New England. An American president – I think it was John F. Kennedy – once stated publicly that the New England men had that honour, which is usually accepted, but Malcolm Jamieson wrote to dispute the statement. The White House conceded, replying with a letter of apology, and said the mistake would not be repeated, all of which clearly tickled Malcolm's well-developed sense of humour, because he roared with laughter as he told me.

Those stout men from Gloucester had links with Berkeley Castle in England, so that is how it came to be named. Unhappily they were all massacred three years later when Indians attacked settlements in Virginia. The place has clearly experienced a disproportionate share of tragedy.

On a happier note (literally!) in one case, Berkeley can claim two more distinctions, quite apart from holding the very first Thanksgiving. During the Union army's destructive occupation in 1862, General Daniel Butterfield, who was stationed there, composed *Taps*, and that haunting bugle call which to this day echoes regularly over military posts all around the world, was first sounded at Berkeley.

The other claim to fame was perhaps a trifle dubious, at least in the opinion of some people. In the very early days, one of the settlers experimented with an alcoholic drink made from Indian corn. It was so palatable that the familiar English ale, brought over at great risk to make the pioneers feel more at home, was refused in its favour.

The front door of the Jamieson residence.

It was the very first bourbon whiskey. And the man who

FOR GOD AND COUNTRY – FOUNDED 1919
ORIGIN OF TAPS
DURING THE CIVIL WAR IN JULY 1862, WHEN THE ARMY OF THE POTOMAC WAS IN CAMP ON THIS SITE, BRIGADIER GENERAL DANIEL BUTTERFIELD SUMMONED PRIVATE OLIVER WILLCOX NORTON, HIS BRIGADE BUGLER, TO HIS TENT. HE WHISTLED SOME NEW TUNE AND ASKED THE BUGLER TO SOUND IT FOR HIM. AFTER REPEATED TRIALS AND CHANGING THE TIME OF SOME NOTES WHICH WERE SCRIBBLED ON THE BACK OF AN ENVELOPE, THE CALL WAS FINALLY ARRANGED TO SUIT GENERAL BUTTERFIELD AND USED FOR THE FIRST TIME THAT NIGHT. FROM THAT TIME IT BECAME AND REMAINS TO THIS DAY THE OFFICIAL CALL FOR "TAPS."
ERECTED BY
THE AMERICAN LEGION
DEPARTMENT OF VIRGINIA
IN TRIBUTE TO
AMERICAN WAR DEAD OF ALL WARS
JULY 4, 1969

'Taps' memorial and inscription (*left*). Painting of General Daniel Butterfield, the composer of 'Taps', under canvas at the Berkeley estate (*right*).

invented it was an episcopalian missionary called George Thorpe, would you believe! Malcolm Jamieson considered that highly amusing, too, and to this day you can acquire bourbon at the Plantation, for he markets his own brand under the Berkeley name. Ten years old and a very fine whiskey – he could personally guarantee it, he said.

I declined his pressing invitation to sample it as cordially as I could, recalling to myself just what it had done to his brave Uncle Walter.

Artist's impression of the invention of Bourbon whisky (*right*). The Berkeley brand of bourbon (*below*).

8

The Confederate Capital – And I Give a Tutorial in English Teamaking

I suppose that the film *Gone With The Wind* will always be the image of the Confederate's challenge to the North in the mind's eye of Britain, and much of the rest of the world. It conveyed such a powerfully romantic portrait, with gleaming white mansions, handsome men with exquisite manners courting elegant young ladies dressed in extravagant gowns, and plump, smiling negro ladies saying 'Lawdy, Miss Scarlett', and rolling their eyes. Richmond was the capital for the Confederacy, and would-be independent nation, and a very prosperous place it is to this day, with many fine buildings – although there was, understandably, a smell of tobacco overhanging the industrial sector. The Virginia leaf has always been pre-eminent in the manufacture of cigarettes, and I suppose much of the city's wealth was originally founded on the world's addiction to nicotine. By the way, I do not belong to the movement which is strenuously opposed to smoking, because, although I have never smoked myself, the smell of tobacco always brings back fond memories of Uncle and his friends gathering around the fire in the kitchen at Low Birk Hatt farm for a chat and a pipe.

One association with Richmond and *Gone With The Wind* was to be found in the hotel where we lodged. The Jefferson was almost a hundred years old and the lobby entrance must be one of the grandest of its kind in the world. It looks like a film set built for a Cecil B. de Mille epic with enormous, marble-effect pillars and a staircase said to be the model for that famous, final

Tea tutorial at Agecroft Hall.

sequence in the film when Rhett Butler told Scarlett O'Hara, that, frankly, he didn't give a damn.

I was taken to see the Southern White House, where the President of the Confederacy, Jefferson Davis, lived and with his Generals planned the South's campaign against the North. The size of the place surprised me, particularly after the impact of the Jefferson Hotel. It was a fairly modest town house with no grounds to speak of. But it had been meticulously restored in every possible detail to exactly the way it was when Mr Davis was resident there. His portrait hangs in the first room you come to, and I couldn't help noticing how much he was like in appearance to his great adversary, Abraham Lincoln. Apparently, I am not the first to remark on this curious coincidence – they could have been brothers. The house has the biggest collection of Confederate memorabilia anywhere in America and I was privileged to be shown the bible that General Robert E. Lee, the Confederate Commander-in-Chief, carried with him – a very precious item. Like Williamsburg, they had gone to the trouble of researching and recreating everything, even down to the fabrics and wallpapers.

The Southern White House in Richmond (*below*), and the Jefferson Davis portrait (*right*).

There was another building I visited in Richmond which had also been recreated, but in an even more dramatic fashion. Agecroft Hall was a Tudor-style manor house built in the eighteenth century – in England! A gentleman called Mr D. C. Williams Jnr., who had made a fortune in tobacco, fell in love with it on a visit to Britain in 1926, the year I was born. He bought it, had it taken down brick by brick, and shipped it to Richmond. There he rebuilt it in twenty-five acres of land with gardens and lawns designed in the English manner, a massive enterprise which cost a fortune. It originally stood in Agecroft, a coal mining area near Manchester, and a beautiful building it was, with oak panelling in many rooms, a minstrel's gallery and a magnificent library. Mr Williams lived there in some style for a time, but eventually his family converted it into a trust and it became a museum.

My difficulty with obtaining a decent pot of tea must have been communicated to the director of Agecroft Hall, Mr Richard Moxley, because he asked me to instruct him and his

Agecroft Hall – a fine old English house.

Richard Moxley's first sip of tea, English style.

staff in the simple art of brewing a decent pot. They had all the necessary equipment, including a magnificent silver tea set and real china which was designed in the classic English manner, and could have been transported across the Atlantic with the house. I went through the routine of warming the pot, and insisted that the water provided was on the boil. This entire tutorial was closely watched, and notes taken, by his staff because they had been considering a proposal to offer visitors to Agecroft Hall a genuine English afternoon tea.

This procedure was obviously a mystery to them, and I was really astonished when Mr Moxley, after pronouncing his first cup delicious, declared that it was the very first time he had ever tasted hot tea. I had noticed that iced tea was very fashionable everywhere I went in the United States, and I did try it myself on a couple of occasions when proper tea of any kind was unobtainable. I half liked one, which I believe was orange and mint flavoured (there were many curious variations), but in the main preferred plain tap water.

There was another taste of home for me in Richmond when I was taken to meet a very lively character called Terry O'Neill. He had arrived from Liverpool thirty years previously and opened an authentic British pub, which he called the Penny Lane. Previously he had been a seafaring man and I was fascinated to learn that he had sailed on the maiden voyage of the QE2. I told him all about my own experiences on board and he searched out a prized memento to show me, a picture of the ship signed by the captain and all the senior crew on that very first crossing of the Atlantic. All the walls in the establishment were adorned in the most patriotic manner, with Union Jacks and portraits of the Royal family everywhere. But there was one corner devoted to the one part of English life that he missed above all others. Liverpool Football Club. He told me he had been a loyal supporter since childhood and lamented that the season just completed had been their worst for many years. He had a network of friends who either posted or personally brought video tapes of Liverpool's matches and other major football events, and on the night I met him the 1993 English Cup Final had just arrived and was being eagerly watched by half a dozen other expatriates in another part of his pub.

Everything about the place was British, right down to the way he spoke, because three decades of life in America had not altered his unmistakable Liverpudlian accent. The food, too, was in the same tradition and I very much enjoyed fish and chips cooked and served exactly the way they are done in England. It was a manageable portion as well, in a country which clearly expects everyone to have an enormous appetite.

There was another gastronomic experience of a contrasting nature when I was taken to meet and have lunch with a leading lady politician in Richmond, Mrs Geline Williams. She was a former mayor of the city and still a member of the council, and very enthusiastic about maintaining the area's links with what she described as the 'mother country'. She told me that her own mother had received a silver medal from the late King George because of her work in organising 'Bundles for Britain' in Richmond during the dark days of the Second World War, before America came to fight with us. They collected clothing, bandages and other items which were in short supply in Britain at the time, and shipped them across. Mrs Williams was a keen supporter of her city's links with Richmond-upon-Thames, with which they have a kind of twinning arrangement, and had paid a couple of visits. I did mention that there was another

Terry O'Neill at the bar of his pub.

MANCHESTER CITY
MAINE ROAD
STRONGBOW
Pink Panther
Soccer Club
WHITBREAD

Richmond – in Yorkshire – and she said she had heard of it and would like to see it one day. The conversation reminded me of the song 'Sweet Lass of Richmond Hill', and the mild controversy surrounding it, as to which of the Richmonds she belonged to.

The meeting was held in a very exclusive place called the Downtown Club, where the prominent businessmen of Richmond meet to discuss and make deals. I had never been so high up in the world, in more ways than one. The club was on the twenty-second floor of a magnificent skyscraper, which gave you a panoramic view of the layout of the city and the river that wends its way through, and I noticed some very pretty wooded hills in the distance. I was informed that Richmond had just overtaken Atlanta in Georgia as the south-eastern headquarters of more of the top five hundred American companies than any other city, which indicated how prosperous the place was.

It was a very elegant occasion which finished in a typically generous way when Mrs Williams presented me with a tankard to mark my stay in Richmond. I only wished I could have responded in like manner, but I didn't even have one of my books to give her. I must remember to send her this one, suitably inscribed.

I was also treated to another slice of 'Living History' before I left Richmond, when I visited a house where the author Edgar Allan Poe had lived for around thirteen years at various times of his life. It is a museum now and the director, Mr Ron Furqueron, had arranged for an actor who bore a remarkable resemblance to Mr Poe to come specially all the way from Baltimore to recite one of Poe's works, dressed in period costume. He was a marvellous performer, but Poe did write some rather bloodcurdling stories and the intensity of the man was quite scary. I sat there, an audience of one, and listened to more than twenty minutes of vintage Poe, sometimes being obliged to close my eyes to shut out some of the more powerful passages. It did not deter him.

My stay in Virginia was a happy and most interesting experience, marred only by a slight scare about my health. I had felt a little unwell for a couple of days and it was thought prudent to seek medical attention. This led swiftly to a visit to hospital for tests, which were remarkable in several ways. To begin with there was little or no privacy, and you were obliged to answer questions of a personal and private nature with

Lunch with Mrs Williams at the Downtown Club.

people passing by. But I was impressed by the speed with which they organised and completed tests which would probably have taken days in Britain. The results were ready in a couple of hours, and thankfully I was pronounced fit and allowed to return to my companions, waiting anxiously at the hotel.

There was one curious incident at hospital. After all the various medical matters had been thoroughly discussed and recorded, I was then cross-examined about our Royal family! They wanted to hear about the problems Prince Charles had been experiencing, but were particularly anxious to obtain the family name of our Royals. Apparently it had been the subject of an animated discussion among the staff, so I was pleased to settle the matter for them by telling them it was Windsor.

9

The Railroad From Hell and Other Minor Problems

On the way to New Orleans.

Travel is delightful, and the latter years of my life, after sixty years of going nowhere, have been wonderfully enhanced by absorbing journeys to several lands. But travel, however careful you are in its organisation, will inevitably mean a certain degree of pain and suffering. The sea will be rough, the train delayed, the plumbing inexplicable, porters unobtainable, luggage mislaid, lifts will try to amputate a limb – the list of potential problems is endless. When you arrive it is usually fine, but getting from place to place is invariably hazardous.

And that is when you are travelling reasonably light. Our little party – just four of us – had twenty-five pieces of television equipment and personal luggage to transport many thousands of miles. Some of the metal cases for camera and sound gear required two strong people to move them, so we were particularly vulnerable. We had many frustrating moments when we toured Europe for the *Innocent Abroad* series and book, mainly connected with having to cross so many borders. Customs officers rarely bothered to check personal luggage, but expensive cameras etc. have to be officially transported on a carnet which creates endless negotiations and confusion. There was only one border to cross on our American Odyssey so we thought that everything would be smooth and orderly by comparison.

And so it was – up to a point. No difficulties with the customs men, and although we were not so innocent as to expect a completely trouble-free time, crises did occur. And always in unexpected ways, when time was short.

To begin with, we anticipated most things in America would be bigger. Most things certainly were, but not in one or two vital areas. Without exception, the vehicles pre-booked for us were not large enough to contain luggage and people, so we were delayed from the first moment we stepped on to American soil from the comfort of the QE2, as described earlier. My hat box disappeared forever at that juncture too.

The next crisis occurred when we moved from New York to Philadelphia, not a vast distance. We were instructed not to take our vehicles (an extra one having been hastily acquired), because there were penalties to pay if you deposited a hired vehicle in another state, so train reservations had been arranged. Having experienced many unpleasant situations travelling by rail in Europe (as related in my book about that trip), a telephone call was made to the station. It yielded some alarming information.

To begin with, luggage accommodation was very limited. And then it turned out that the train stopped for three minutes in New York and a similar time in Philadelphia. That is plenty when you have the normal complement of luggage, but how do you shift twenty-five pieces weighing upwards of half a ton in one hundred and eighty seconds? So Barry Cockcroft asked the concierge at the Plaza Hotel to arrange a driver and a vehicle big enough to accommodate us. And a 32-seater bus turned up! It was explained that there was nothing in between that and an inadequate van. We felt we should have gone out and tried to sell one-way tickets to Philadelphia, because we made a slightly ridiculous sight setting off with just four passengers and a driver. And it cost four hundred dollars, not including the tip – and tipping was to be one of our major expenses throughout. Consternation was the order of the day whenever we turned up at a hotel, with porters staring in disbelief at the load we were proposing to bring in. Nothing could be left in the vehicle because of the high value of television gear and the danger of theft. Fortunately, our rooms were generally large enough to cope with the volume, but it usually took a long time and many ten dollar bills, sometimes twenties, were pressed into sweating palms before we were settled. One porter even remarked that he had spent less energy moving furniture into a new apartment a couple of days before!

There were other small irritations along the way, usually associated with vehicles, but the real nightmare happened when we made the thousand-mile-plus hop from Virginia to New Orleans. At least, it was supposed to begin from Virginia but another timely phone call prevented an impossible situation developing yet again, because we were told our train stayed in Charlottesville, the intended point of embarkation, for only around seven minutes. This meant we had to go all the way back to Washington, DC, where it was guaranteed to stop for over half an hour. The Virginia State Tourist Board, which had provided a fifteen-seater bus – the perfect transport – and a very efficient and friendly coloured driver called Eugene (I wish we could have taken him all the way with us), kindly allowed us to take it to Washington.

Now we certainly had plenty of time to unload all the gear and luggage, and several porters to assist when we arrived at Washington's palatial railway station. But when we boarded the train we found we had nowhere to put it except in the luggage van, and we had had strict instructions not to let it out of our sight – it was far too risky, and the painful memory of all of our possessions being re-routed part of the way to Moscow during a railway journey to Cologne on our last overseas tour was still with us. There had obviously been a mistake. We had been booked into what are called roomettes – slightly less commodious than monks' cells, and measuring around seven feet by six foot six inches.

We had been lulled into a false sense of security due to Barry Cockcroft's previous experience of the American railway system, which had been entirely pleasurable. He had told us about the gleaming silver double deckers boasting grand pianos, restaurants, bars and all the space you could wish for. And he said that even the older rolling stock had bedrooms which opened up into suites big enough for a double bed.

With Barry Cockcroft in the dining car.

By tradition, we travelled first class. Mostly for the benefit of the programmes because the contrast between, say, a suite at the Plaza and a flashback to the rather spartan conditions in which I lived at Low Birk Hatt farm made a more telling sequence; and partly because the more expensive the accommodation the more room we could expect to house our impedimenta. But there had been a breakdown in communications somewhere and we were stuck with the roomettes. Nor could we do anything about it. An attempt was made to move up to the larger rooms, but they were all booked solid. One extra roomette was available, which was snapped up, and then negotiations were opened up to change one of our cells for a larger variety meant for a disabled person. We succeeded in the end and I was rather glad, because it had superior toilet facilities. You see, each roomette had its own WC, not exactly a savory arrangement in so confined a space, and when you pulled the bed down it was entirely covered. If you had need to use the WC during the night you had to push back the bed, which would have been too much for me because of the weight. So at least I had the use of a disabled room thankfully free of this restriction, which was a step or two away from my own, although I had to negotiate my way through a mountain of our metal boxes. There was also very little room for manoeuvre in the corridors, particularly in the sleeping car section. Several large ladies and gentlemen – and there were many on that crowded journey, which I imagine was a direct consequence of the enormous quantity of food served up as a matter of course in America – had real difficulty trying to progress along the train. One heard many exclamations, such as 'Lawdy Me!', and it was often necessary for people to ask permission to step into your roomette to relieve the log jam.

But all this amounted to a passing inconvenience. The real blow, which affected the rest of the trip, happened when Barry Cockcroft – in the general frustration, indeed real anger, surrounding the operation – hauled one heavy case too many and sustained an injury. He said nothing to me at the time, nor for some days, but confided in the others. This meant we were down to just two people – Mostafa and Chris – to do the heavy lifting from then on.

The journey lasted for more than twenty-four hours. The boys called it The Railroad From Hell, but that must not be construed as an indictment of the railway company. They were not responsible for our need to carry so much weight. Nor were they to blame for the delays, caused partly by a mechanical fault and partly because one passenger suffered a heart attack during the night, so an emergency stop had to be made with ambulances and police turning up. We were told that happily the man was still alive when they got him to hospital. But it was an ill-fated train.

I could not fault the staff or the catering arrangements, and I would not hesitate to recommend this particular route to anyone travelling with just personal luggage. The train manager was very attentive and came to apologise to us personally, saying that the task was not easy because the carriages had been built almost fifty years ago and were well worn, and certainly inferior to those on the other routes. Definitely not suitable for television crews with roomettes. But the food was palatable and we did see more remarkable sights as we rolled through places like Lynchburg, Atlanta in Georgia, Birmingham in Alabama, a place with the charming name of Tuscaloosa (named after an Indian chief), and Picayune. I did notice that the deeper South we travelled the more the homes visible from the train became less appealing. Indeed, some were little better than shacks. I suppose no one who can afford

A glimpse of the houses near the track.

Crossing the causeway to New Orleans.

better would choose to live in a house close to a railway line, but it was obvious to me that most if not all of those living in these reduced circumstances were coloured people.

We also went through some dense forest, and as we approached Louisiana we travelled through what I can only describe as swamp land, with some unusual trees growing out of the water. But the last six miles of that tedious journey proved to be the most interesting – if somewhat unnerving. The train crosses a causeway over Lake Pontchartarin, six hundred and thirty square miles of fresh water leading directly to the skyscrapers of New Orleans. Once you are on the

causeway no land or supports can be seen on either side, so I imagine it must be a single track. It was a queer feeling, and the train went so slowly I wondered if the driver had to be careful to avoid creating vibrations which could lead to us tipping over.

But it must have been a feat to build a railway line across six miles of water, and it was a most unusual way to enter New Orleans. I saw herons flying alongside the carriage and glimpsed jetties and fishermen's homes on stilts. They were all illuminated by a beautiful sunset. So it was a romantic arrival, if nothing else.

10

New Orleans and the Mighty Mississippi

Two things strike you on entering New Orleans – the heat and the noise. Emerging from the station is like stepping into a slow oven, and the humidity was high enough to drain your energy after only a short walk. And every few yards in the French quarter your eardrums were assaulted by music. Jazz, of course. Not that I am complaining because I love music of every variety, but it could be a trifle overwhelming.

For me, perhaps, the greatest attraction of this classic place was the Mississippi. I had read about the mighty river, listened to songs about it, but nothing prepares you for its sheer majesty. It curves around the centre of New Orleans in a huge crescent and it is full of the most varied traffic, from mundane barges being pushed in long lines by tugs, to magnificent paddle steamers straight out of the last century. One of the greatest pleasures during my stay was to sit in my hotel room and watch the activity. I was staying in an enormous suite at the Windsor Court, which had just been nominated the hotel of the year in America. It was owned by the same company that operated the Orient Express, one of the fondest memories of my trip to Europe. If only that sublime train had been running from Washington, DC to New Orleans . . .

The Windsor Court was an English-style oasis, with portraits of racehorses and royalty everywhere and a large statue of Saint George at the entrance. There was a portrait of King George V and Queen Mary, with her familiar choker,

The paddle steamer 'Creole Queen' leaving New Orleans.

something you rarely see even in England. The hotel was situated at the edge of the French quarter and very handy for our frequent trips to sample the excitement on offer. Believe me, there's no place I know which matches the energy of New Orleans. It was always like a boiling kettle, twenty-four hours a day, with the streets full of tourists and itinerant performers, the latter trying to persuade the former to part with their change. Clowns, quick sketch artists, balloon sculptors, Charlie Chaplin clones, dancers, and musicians of all kinds could be seen on every street corner, and I marvelled at their ability to stand the heat. Some wore heavy and elaborate costumes so they must have shed pounds every day.

Most visitors have a set pattern or a list of objectives when they visit New Orleans in order to sample as many of the unique attractions as possible. First you may proceed to Jackson Square, the gateway to the French quarter, and take the view from the steps leading down from the levee on the side of the Mississippi. The levees, huge raised banks, are essential to prevent flooding because the city is below sea level. Then it is customary to go to a corner café in the square to have *beignets* and *café au lait* – the place was originally owned by the

Afro hairstyle in New Orleans.

A view of Jackson Square and the Cathedral.

French and the language is still used. It was sold to the newly-independent America by Napoleon Bonaparte, who wanted the money to finance his war against Britain. The Louisiana Purchase was an historic landmark for America because it doubled the size of the fledgeling nation and only cost them around three cents an acre. Most of the money, oddly enough, was borrowed from Britain. Napoleon proved to be the all-round loser since he spent the money on building the army which lost to Wellington at Waterloo.

The city was originally named in honour of the Duke of Orléans, and the French influence is reflected in the food on offer – mixed with Cajun and Creole cooking which is very spicy. *Beignets* are made from a batter, deep fried, dipped in icing sugar and served hot. I quite liked them, but the sugar was so light it floated all over the place and ended up in my hair and clothes. Very difficult to brush off, too. Whilst I was eating them, entertainment came at me from all angles, with a very skilful trumpet player performing on one side, a clown amusing the children on the other, and a man in strange attire who sneaked up behind passers by and mimicked their walk and other characteristics. I didn't care for him because his humour was based on ridicule, and some of his victims were

A close up of the famous beignets.

Café au lait and beignets in Jackson Square. . .

. . . with a trumpet accompaniment.

not at all pleased. The trumpet player I really appreciated. An enterprising fellow he was, because he had postcards of himself, and even tapes of his recordings for sale.

Traditionally, the next thing to do seemed to be to take a ride in an open carriage around the network of famous streets leading out of Jackson Square. I declined, having had my fill of that kind of transport in New York, Williamsburg and with the Amish, but I was interested to see that some of the animals were mules. They were all decorated with flowers and bells and pompoms and a few of them were wearing hats to protect their heads against the fierce heat. I was content to walk, which was quite pleasant if you were careful to stick to the shade, but frequent stops for drinks to counter the steady loss of body fluids were absolutely necessary. The fashionable thing to do at this point would have been to order something called a Hurricane. It's a large and colourful mixture with a rum base and probably rather lethal so I just stuck to Adam's Ale, which is how we described water in Baldersdale.

Keeping my distance from a Hurricane!

There was much to beguile the eye along the streets of the French quarter, and I was particularly struck by the architecture. Many buildings had balconies, fringed by decorative ironwork, and were obviously very old. Some had hammocks slung from the ceiling or were very colourfully decorated. Street life was fascinating, and every few yards there was someone trying to persuade you to enter their café or club, or offering something for sale. There were also regular opportunities to have your shoes polished, which is obviously a popular service in America because I had noticed shoeshine men in hotel lobbies, railway stations and street corners everywhere along my American journey. I fell into conversation with one who was plying his trade in St Peter Street, in the heart of the jazz sector. He had a badge in his hat which proclaimed him to be a veteran of the Vietnam War, and he had a good sense of humour balanced with a certain sadness. Jerry Evans was his name and he was very precise about the length of his service in Vietnam – two years, five months and fourteen days. That was indicative of something, probably the pain and fear of it, but he didn't elaborate, save to say that he fought with the Fifth Group Special Forces, a Green Beret unit which I understand is equivalent to our Royal Marine Commandos. So he must have been involved in some unpleasant business. He also said he was a retired chef, but all he did now was shine shoes and chase women! I did wonder

In the heart of the jazz quarter – note the intricate ironwork on the balconies.

PIZZA
& PASTA
PRESERVATION
HALL
PATIO

Soles of the tap dancers' footwear (*above*).

why a man like him was now obliged to shine shoes to eke out a living, but I thought it impolite to enquire. He said that he met people from all around the world and they all received a big welcome in New Orleans because it was such a friendly place. According to him, the tensions that often exist between black and white people were rare in his city. There were few social barriers and they mixed happily – as demonstrated by a humorous story he told me about himself and a black friend. Apparently their favourite bar is mainly frequented by white people but they go there regularly and always have a good time even though the two of them look, as he put it, like 'flies in a bowl of milk'!

Round the corner I noticed two coloured boys hoping to part the tourists from a copper or two by dancing at a furious rate. They obviously couldn't afford proper tap shoes, so they had jammed beer bottle tops and other bits of metal to the soles of their trainers. One couldn't have been more than seven or eight years old, and we recorded them for the series for which they received a handsome sum. But there was an unpleasant moment when we were moving away from the boys, because a man appeared claiming to be their father and demanding money for himself. From the mystified look on the youngsters' faces I would guess they had never seen him before.

Jazz, of course, is the very heart and soul of New Orleans. From lunchtime onwards until the early hours, scores of bands swing into operation, and a walk down Bourbon Street could leave you dizzy. First I went with the crowds swirling around the principal shrine in the French quarter, a placed called Preservation Hall in St Peter Street where jazz is said to have originated. What they certainly have not preserved with any care is the hall itself, because the woodwork had been a stranger to paint for many years and the windows did not seem to have been cleaned for as long. There was a cockroach crawling along one pane. If this was deliberate policy, to give the place an aged and historic look, then they had succeeded one hundred per cent. I returned to Preservation Hall during the evening, but the place was jammed with an enthusiastic crowd so I joined the group listening at that greasy window. It was as far as I wanted to go, and not just because of the heat and the crush of perspiring humanity, but because the music they were playing – to an ecstatic reception, I have to admit – was too loud for me and dominated by a man playing a set of drums by the window. In my opinion, the drums should be used sparingly, if at all. I went round the corner of Bourbon

Jerry Evans, the shoeshine man (*left*).

Through the window of Preservation Hall.

Street in search of something more to my taste.

Earlier that day I had spent a pleasant hour listening to a solo piano player in a hotel called The Inn on Bourbon Street. People sat with their drinks on a ledge built around the shape of the piano, an unusual but practical arrangement, and the musician was very friendly and talked to all the customers. When told I was from England, he actually played 'God Save The Queen', which meant I had to stand up along with our sound recordist, Chris, who was with me at the time. I think the others were slightly taken aback at this small demonstration of loyalty, but it happened spontaneously. When we left they were playing a song only vaguely familiar to me, all about leaving by ship for England's green and pleasant shores.

I was tempted to go back there in the evening but I thought I couldn't come to New Orleans and not listen to a live jazz band for an hour or so. I walked most of the length of Bourbon Street and considered and rejected many establishments because of the raucous sounds issuing from their doors. You would need cotton wool in your ears to bear the volume in many of those

The solo pianist at the Inn on Bourbon Street.

places. Finally, to my relief, I chanced upon a place where the group was playing my kind of music – by that I mean the original Dixieland jazz; slower and more melodic numbers. No drums or strident saxophones, just classic jazz of the quieter kind.

There was a very unexpected finale to that evening, my last in New Orleans, because as midnight approached in Bourbon Street I heard cries of 'Hannah, Hannah', and a group of British folk came rushing across the street to greet me. They were from Bradford, and they were closely followed by two other parties, one from Barnsley and the other from Newcastle. There must have been about a dozen of them altogether. We had a nice chat about our respective experiences in America and they took a lot of photographs. One of the gentlemen had a little video camera, so for a time there were two trained on me because Mostafa and Chris were also busily recording the greetings.

So I'd had my fill of jazz and the other attractions of the French quarter, but there was still a gap in my list of essentials.

A trip on the mighty Mississippi.

A couple of very handsome boats were offering rides to the

public from the riverside near our hotel. But the Delta Steamboat Company said that if they were to compete in style and size with the QE2, then I must drive for an hour or so, deeper into Louisiana to Baton Rouge, to board the *Mississippi Queen*.

It was the biggest paddle steamer in the world and had been created, would you believe, by the same man who designed the QE2. Obviously a most talented person.

Like the First Lady of the Atlantic, the first glimpse of the *Mississippi Queen* quite took your breath away. It had five decks, two towering smoke stacks and was entirely steam powered, just as in the days when Mark Twain wrote his *Huckleberry Finn* stories.

As you stepped on board this magnificent vessel your imagination went back in time to an age of adventure, with ladies in crinoline skirts and gamblers in brocaded waistcoats

Night scene from my hotel window – a river boat arrives (*above*).

About to board the Mississippi Queen (*above right*).

A meeting with 'Mark Twain' (*right*).

and all kinds of colourful characters. I walked round the vessel as it steamed along what I've always thought to be the most romantic river in America, took tea in the lounge and sat by the giant red paddles as they churned up the dense waters. I even had a personal meeting with Mark Twain himself – in reality a retired State Trooper, who had become a recognised authority on the legendary author. He dressed in the fashion of his character, wore a wig to add more authenticity, and we had a most interesting conversation.

There was music everywhere too, a full jazz band in the lounge, a very talented pianist in one of the bars and the most curious instrument I have yet encountered in America. It was placed outside on the very top of the boat and called a calliope. Similar to an organ but powered entirely by steam, it was traditionally played whenever the *Mississippi Queen* left its mooring. Navigating such an enormous boat powered only by steam demands a great deal of talent and experience of the currents and sandbanks, as the Mississippi can be treacherous. I thought it most heartening that someone was prepared to invest so much time, effort and money in keeping such a fascinating part of America's history alive.

11

Cajun Country – Alligators, Snapping Turtles and Greg Guirard

Aerial view of the Atchafalaya Basin.

From New Orleans and the Mississippi my route pushed further into the very heart of Louisiana where there is even more water, immense natural beauty and a definite hint of danger. It is called Cajun Country.

You really do leave the modern world behind when you enter this very special area, for it is inhabited by a people that are like no other in the vast continent of America. They are basically fisherfolk, who arrived here from Canada several generations ago. They have a very distinctive culture, which appears not to have been diffused, like others, by the passage of time and integration with other ways of life. Their music is unique, so is their food, and their first language is a version of French. They do not work the sea, although the Gulf of Mexico is only fifty miles away and there is access from the Mississippi. They work the bayous in the immense swampland which is blessed in many ways. They are quite isolated and no doubt this helped them keep a distance between themselves and the mainstream of life.

I had a guide through Cajun Country: a man who has acquired an international reputation for his writing and photography, and his campaign to protect the land where he lives and works from the ravages of modern society. Of all the many fine people I met in the United States, Greg Guirard is probably the one I admired the most. He was a true countryman, quiet, modest, and considerate, but strong in mind and body and absolutely sure of himself and his cause.

Greg's grandfather lived, worked and hunted in the wilderness of the Atchafalaya Basin, and Greg himself had lived on its western edge since the age of two. He is an authority on the area and the Cajun people, and he told me how they had come to live in the swampland. He said they were originally French, mainly from Normandy and Brittany,

Touring the swamps with Greg Guirard.

who had emigrated to the Novia Scotia and New Brunswick areas of Eastern Canada in the long distant past. France and England fought over these territories from the seventeenth century onwards, and when the English finally won control they demanded that the French settlers either swear allegiance to the Crown or leave. Most refused, and were shipped out – some back to France, others to the Caribbean and Florida – but one group, mainly fishermen, headed for Louisiana. That was two hundred years ago, and now it is estimated that there are around three quarters of a million Cajun people in Louisiana.

When they arrived, their forefathers had to face up not only to the challenge of making a new life but to certain unusual dangers from the local wildlife, which still threaten the unwary or foolhardy today. For lurking in the waters are alligators, snapping turtles and poisonous snakes. Greg himself has had some nasty moments with water moccasin snakes, but alligators seem to pose the greater threat. Although they are smaller and less ferocious than their African cousins, the crocodile, one male alligator in the swamp grew to a length of nineteen feet two inches and weighed just under a ton. The smaller females are all around ten feet in length and they all generally try to stay out of the way of humans. But they are hunted for their skins and for the table, particularly the younger, more tender variety, and they can obviously defend themselves and their young. They are lightning fast according to Greg, and swifter than a man over clear ground. They do hunt other species, and are particularly fond of pigs. Apparently, they lie just under the water in places where pigs come to drink, spring out and seize them by their tails as they turn to run. I was sad to hear that many dogs end up as alligator snacks, even if due to their own foolishness. They tend to leap around barking at alligators lying totally motionless and seemingly oblivious to them, which is of course encouragement to come nearer. Greg said that alligators can strike as quickly as a snake and dogs have no chance.

Snapping turtles are much prized and therefore valuable delicacies; and they can also put up a good fight. They live underwater and are hunted by men who dive sometimes to a depth of ten feet without the benefit of bottled air. When the hunter locates one, the trick is to hold his breath and gingerly feel the shell of the turtle with his feet. He can then ascertain from the position of horns on the shell which end has the dangerous bit – the head. He can then grab him in a safe manner and haul him ashore. Make a mistake and you can lose a piece of yourself, for apparently when a snapping turtle bites he will never let go.

Greg told me a story about a turtle-hunting expedition that went wrong. It seemed totally unbelievable, but came from one of his close friends who swore he personally witnessed what I am about to tell you when he turned up one day at a doctor's surgery after stepping on a rusty nail. There was someone else waiting for the doctor to arrive with a much more urgent problem. He was holding a ten pound snapping turtle which had his nose firmly locked in its jaws! It seems this man had been checking one of his underwater turtle traps by diving

The hazards of the bayous . . . an alligator.
. . . snapping turtle.
. . . water snake, with snack.

Cajun fishermen with a day's haul, including my favourite catfish (*above right*). Turtle fishermen (*right*).

AMBAR

down and sticking his head in to have a look. You can imagine the rest.

It was taking some time for the doctor to turn up and the man suddenly said that he had to have a cigarette. So he held the turtle in his left hand and, dripping blood, lit a cigarette with the other. Greg's friend said that as long as he lived he never expected to see a more bizarre sight than that. Eventually the doctor appeared and cut off the turtle's head which released the muscles and freed his nose, which probably never recovered from the experience.

I understand why people take such risks to catch turtles, because people all over the world will pay huge sums to make soup from their meat; and I know that the skins of alligators go to make very expensive and valuable shoes and handbags. But I was surprised to learn how many restaurants in Louisiana offered alligator steaks on their menus, since alligators are now protected and you must have a licence to hunt them. Maybe the authorities turn a blind eye to a little illegal hunting (and there was plenty of poaching in my own Baldersdale). Perhaps it was allowed to help the tourist industry, because I suppose lots of people would like to go home and tell their friends they had eaten alligator. But I allowed the opportunity to pass by. Greg said that various parts of the beast had different tastes ranging from chicken to pork, and that they were all very palatable.

I ate a meal with Greg in a typical Cajun restaurant which was full of local families on a night out, and had a marvellous, genuine atmosphere. Large groups, ranging from the elderly to the very young, sat around extended tables, mostly eating from giant pans full of bright red crawfish and listening to a band playing traditional Cajun music, which is something like a cross between traditional French and Country and Western. They also liked to dance and even that had a style of its own, a cross between the two-step and a waltz. Large rolls of kitchen paper were strategically placed on every table since you had to get to personal grips with a crawfish. You eat their tails, which are two or three inches long, and they look like miniature lobsters. I chose catfish, as I had been introduced to them in New Orleans. Catfish will be my chief gastronomic memory of America. It is very choice indeed, having a firm, clear white flesh – very similar to a large, plump plaice – but I have no idea how it got it's name. Apparently they are abundant throughout Louisiana and some of the neighbouring states of the deep

Steamed crawfish.

Crawfish in 42 lb sacks ready for market.

South, and I even ate and enjoyed some cooked in Cajun spices.

Greg makes part of his living from catching crawfish. He leads a double life in the economic sense, leaving his home in the morning to haul in his traps in the swamps and baiting them again before returning. On a good day, each trap will yield between six and eight pounds of crawfish and Greg sets a total of two hundred and twenty traps. He said that every year one hundred thousand million pounds of crawfish are harvested in Louisiana, and that the 1993 season had been the best in living memory. Consequently, however, the price had dropped to twenty-five cents a pound from a high of seventy-five cents, and he certainly wasn't getting rich even with his large daily catch. And he even had to pay twenty-one cents a pound for his bait!.

Apparently, even crawfishing has its penalties. Because even though they only weigh around six ounces, crawfish can develop large claws later on in the season and protective gloves need to be worn. They are cumbersome and get in the way and are often discarded, and it is easy to spot a crawfisherman who takes that risk, because his hands will resemble two half-pounds of minced beef.

Greg spends the other half of his day writing, taking photographs and collecting driftwood from the swamps to make into furniture and wall decorations. He was extremely well educated, and the possessor of a degree from Louisiana State University in Baton Rouge. For years he had been a teacher but he resigned because the pay was so poor and the call of the bayous so strong.

In the course of a varied career, he says he has lived in three countries other than the United States, and three states other than Louisiana, and has seen many beautiful and wonderful things. But to his mind nothing can compare with his homeland, the Atchafalaya Basin, because there was something magical there which feeds the spirit.

He showed me round his house which was a delightful old place situated in woodland, totally isolated and full of curiosities such as an American Elm Tree he has allowed to grow through the floor of his conservatory. The roof leaks when it rains, which is a natural consequence, and he regularly had to cut away the floorboards to allow room for the trunk to expand, but he considered it well worthwhile. Greg began the tour by showing me some of the photographs and the superb

With Greg Guirard at his house.

books he has published, which have been described by one literary critic as 'a love letter from a man to his place'. Another writer called his photographs 'poetic masterpieces', and I have to say I agree. Greg is dismissive of all this praise; he says he creates the books solely to increase people's awareness of the value of the bayous, and to lessen the chances of them being changed into something less beautiful and less wild.

He also states that in his opinion photography is not an art. A claim that I am certain Mostafa Hammuri would strenuously oppose!

I was concerned about his isolation, for he is separated from his wife, and wondered what he would do if he became ill or had an accident. But he told me that there was a ninety-four-year-old woman living alone deep in the swamp, and if she could risk it, so could he. When he first came to live by the bayou he was two years old and his house was just an old cabin with no access by road. It could only be reached by boat.

Everything – the house and all the furniture – was made of cypress wood which used to be plentiful in the bayous in the old days but is, sadly, today non-existent. In the late eighteenth century, and throughout most of the nineteenth, loggers cut down every one, it seems. It is fashionable now to lament about the destruction of the rain forests in South America, but in the swamps of Louisiana it amounted to total anihilation. Greg said they chopped down every last one, and his books press home the tragedy of it. Nobody had the wisdom to preserve any, or to replant. His only sources of cypress wood to work nowadays are the logs, lost or discarded generations ago, which float on or under the water. Greg had salvaged an entire barnful. Many of them are two thousand years old, and Greg said that although young Cypress trees are sprouting everywhere, not even his grandchildren would see the full glory of the bayous because it would take another two thousand years before they could be fully restored.

I was reminded at that moment of the words of the song: 'Poems are made by fools like me, but only God can make a tree.'

Ironically, Greg's own grandfather, Wade O. Martin senior, born in 1885, was one of those responsible for the disappearance of the trees. He owned thirteen hundred acres of forest which fed his sawmill. Greg obviously loved his grandfather, who used to take him hunting and camping, and taught him the ways of the wilderness; his finest book is dedicated to him, along with an author who had also inspired him, William Faulkner.

Greg is now trying as best as he can to repair the damage done by his grandfather. He inherited one hundred of his acres, which were growing cash crops such as sugar cane and corn. Resisting the advice of his family, he has spent the last seventeen years turning it back to the forest it once was. He has planted thirty thousand trees, more than fifteen varieties, including cypress and oak. It may be too late for his grandchildren, but he says that one day it will be a haven for wildlife, and a place where people can seek peace and tranquility.

All in all, a true measure of the man's commitment and passion for nature.

Finally, Greg gave me a tour of the place he holds so dear. We boarded a flat-bottomed boat and sailed out into almost one million acres of wetlands. It is controlled by man to prevent the

Cypress trees in the sunset.

low lying cities of Baton Rouge and Lafayette from flooding. A vast system of levees and locks regulate the water flowing into the swamp from the Mississippi, built after a disastrous flood in 1927 which partly submerged many towns and villages in the area. The depth of the water also changes with the seasons. There can be a twenty foot difference between spring and autumn, and during the time I spent around the bayous Greg estimated an average depth of six to ten feet. Several parts of the swamp have trees growing out of the water – quite thickly in parts – and I thought what an unusual experience it was to travel through a forest in a boat. There are a few varieties of tree which would thrive with their feet in water, including cypress and a species of willow. Every now and then I would see the massive stumps of the giant trees the loggers had cut down, memorials to a past splendour.

A beaver at his lodge.

I was taken to view a beaver lodge but there was nobody at home at the time, nor did we see any of the otters which lived there in numbers. Greg said that although the beavers behaved themselves, otters were not too popular with fishermen because they had a habit of raiding the crawfish traps, and opening up fifty or sixty at a time. The place was teeming with fish at all times, and was a favourite place for sport fishermen trying for a big fish such as bass, as well as those who made a living at it like Greg. He described a method used by one man to catch fish which seemed rather extreme to me. He puts out a net 1,700 feet long called a Travelling Seine, which floats on the surface but has sides which go all the way down to the bottom, and when it is hauled in no fish in the huge circle it has created stands a chance. Apparently catches of five thousand to six thousand pounds can be achieved in this way. It seemed to me that this would do to the fish what the loggers did to the big cypress trees if it wasn't controlled.

The young trees succeeding the cypresses are very handsome, and as we progressed deeper into the swamp we saw Spanish moss hanging in swathes from the branches, a truly splendid sight. I thought at first that Spanish moss was a

A great egret in flight.

parasite which may retard the growth of the trees, but Greg said it was an air plant, and harmless. In the past it had yielded a useful income on the side to the Cajuns. It was used as upholstery for furniture, being very light and springy when dried out. Thousands of tons were harvested every year in the past, but Greg told me it had to be done very carefully because small poisonous snakes and even wasps used to nest in it. The invention of foam rubber finished that enterprise, although there was still a small demand, for use in decorative purposes.

At this point I heard a very romantic, sad legend, concerning the origins of Spanish moss. It is said that a beautiful Indian maiden with long hair died tragically just before her wedding day, and her would-be bridegroom cut off her hair and let it blow away in the wind. It settled in the branches of the swamp and began to grow . . .

My senses were overwhelmed that day by the sheer beauty and tranquility of the place. We floated through a carpet of water hyacinths, white and lilac in colour and so thick it seemed possible to step out of the boat and walk on them. They were first brought here one hundred years ago from Japan and have flourished ever since, blooming all through the summer

The houseboat with indoor fishing facilities.

and beyond until the frost gets to them in November. We also saw the occasional houseboat tucked away in the foliage, including one very ancient looking construction which had an unusual facility. The owner, an old swamp dweller, had cut a trap door in one cabin so he could fish in bad weather without having to go outside. He had also decorated the exterior very attractively with pieces of old cypress wood dredged from the water. Greg explained how the sand flowing year after year in the currents wore away the sap wood leaving just the hard centre. The shapes created by nature in this way were very artistic.

We didn't see any alligators which didn't bother me, but Greg said they would certainly be around somewhere. They didn't appear much during the day, and generally avoided humans so the danger they presented was negligible unless you disturbed their nesting grounds. But at night you could spot them quite easily by shining a torch, because their red eyes reflected the light. A sight which would be calculated to freeze the marrow of a nervous character like me. Problems did occur when locals put out food for the alligators for the benefit of the tourists, because if you happened to turn up at one of the feeding spots with nothing to give them, they may become aggressive.

The day concluded with one of the most awe inspiring sunsets I have ever seen. Even Greg was impressed, and became very busy with his camera. The boat's engine was cut and for nearly an hour we drifted through the hyacinths and the trees dripping with Spanish moss, watching large white egrets flapping slowly over water turned into rippling, golden silk by the last rays of the sun.

Altogether an experience that will remain in my memory permanently.

A superb sunset over the bayou.

12

Houston, Texas – and My Close Encounter with the Moon

Texas, at last. This was the place which I had mentally put at the top of my list right from the start. But first of all I was taken to see the Texas of tomorrow, not the one my generation had seen when they went to see the cowboy films on the cinema screen.

Houston, which is the fourth largest city in America, turned out to have a skyline just as overwhelming as New York's. Indeed, I would venture to say that the architecture in Houston was even more breathtaking than that of New York, probably because the centre was built at a later date, and the designers had a chance to be more imaginative. The shape to some of these towering structures was remarkable, ranging from wedding-cake to ultra modern; and the use of a covering which makes them appear to be made of metallic glass is very widespread. I later discovered that although you cannot see into the building from outside, you could look out from inside. Very clever.

Personally, I reached heights never attained before when I was placed in a room on the twenty-seventh floor of our hotel. The ride up was a trial every time because one set of lifts had a glass side looking out on to the lobby, and the others were even worse because the view was of the street outside. I used to grit my teeth, close my eyes and shut it out of my mind. It was, of course, another example of American ingenuity, although I felt in that case it was purely for dramatic effect and served no practical purpose. But then for many years, America has led

The skyline of Houston in the distance.

View from the 27th floor (*above*).

The fearful lifts at the Hyatt Regency Hotel (*right*).

The extravagant skyscrapers of Houston (*left*).

Dwarfed by Saturn Five.

the world in technological matters, and nowhere was this more evident than in Houston. Because it was here, at the NASA Headquarters, that America's space programme sent men to the moon for the very first time. The rockets may have been launched from Florida, but it was all controlled from NASA in Houston, and all the astronauts were trained there. Now they have created a Space Center (that's the way they spell 'centre'), and it was here that I had my close encounter with the moon.

The approach to the Space Center was a spectacle in itself, because they had parked a variety of space vehicles there which you could walk round and inspect. One, the Saturn Five rocket, seemed to be nearly a quarter of a mile long and the size of the engines was awesome. Inside the vast buildings I was given a guided tour, starting with a mock up of a space lab where the astronauts were taught to cope with weightlessness. I saw a very lifelike model of a man spinning around, clutching his knees. There was another one taking a shower in a plastic bag, a necessary thing because if water splashed on to the

The gigantic engines of Saturn Five.

machinery there could have been serious consequences. Then I was taken to see a display recreating the historic moon landing, with more realistic models of astronauts and their moon buggy on the lunar surface, and the earth visible in the distance. It appeared to be a very desolate and wintry scene to me with Mother Earth so far away – more than a quarter of a million miles, I was told. At that point I wondered if those brave men ever looked at it and feared they would never get back home. But I was glad to hear that they did all return safely.

Next to the display was the actual command module of Apollo 17 which had been to the moon and back, and looked somewhat battered by the experience. In fact, it was the last

one to do so, and that was in 1972. Three men had flown in it, and I told my guide that it was to be hoped they had been compatible, because it must have been very cramped.

Apollo 17 – the last capsule on the moon.

My conclusion to the visit to the Space Center was a trifle unsettling, in a rather strange way. In one special room, under glass and closely guarded, was a piece of the moon which had been brought back on Apollo 17. It was a small, slender, triangular-shaped slice of smooth black rock, and they had left just enough room in the reinforced glass container to slide your hand in to touch it. I was rather loathe to do so at first – I cannot explain why – but I finally gave it a pat. Personally, I still prefer to keep a quarter of a million miles between myself and the moon. The room itself was a high-security vault. I was told that moon rocks were so precious, because a lot of research had still

A close encounter with the moon.

to be completed, that they were kept in a building which was proofed against earthquakes and hurricanes. Apparently, NASA scientists are still planning to establish a community in space, and I informed my guide that I would not be on the list of applicants.

Later that day, I did my own bit of space travel in that hotel lift, and came across a sad story which demonstrated how much effort was still required to put things to rights on earth, before we try to colonise the other planets. We were having some of the heavy equipment moved, and the porter sent to do the job was Cuban by birth. After the hauling around was finished and he had paused to get his breath back (I always felt sorry for the porters we encountered), we had a friendly conversation. He said his family once owned a major hardware store in Havana, which had the sole distribution rights for some lines of American goods. But this particular advantage obviously did them no good at all when Fidel Castro came to power, because he seized the business and sent the man's father to prison. What really upset him and the rest of the family more than anything was the fact that his sister had been one of Castro's revolutionary supporters, and didn't change her position when they jailed her father who, he said, died prematurely as a result. He himself had escaped to America, and considered himself fortunate, because, although he may have lost his inheritance and the chance of a comfortable life, he didn't go hungry. And Cuba was apparently in such a dreadful state, with shortages of all essential goods following the collapse of Russian aid and the continuing hostility from America, which had banned all trade, that he was getting pitiful appeals for help from his cousins still living there. I suppose in Britain we tend to regard the situation in Cuba with an open mind, since we are not directly involved. Castro did get rid of a dictator, but for all his revolutionary ideals it seems that one extreme regime was replaced by another – a case of out of the frying pan and into the fire, in my estimation.

I encountered more sadness from the past in Houston when I visited the San Jacinto Monument on the outskirts of the city; although it had led to a new and better future (I suppose Castro would say the same about Cuba). It was here, in 1836, that the state of Texas was born. Indeed, it had been the Republic of Texas for ten years, a completely independent nation. Texas used to belong to Mexico and was quite content to be a colony until General Santa Anna and a group of corrupt Mexican politicians made life unbearable for the Texans. So they went to war, and Texas won the opening skirmishes. This enraged Santa Anna, a very cruel man, who decided to take no prisoners. When four hundred Texans were obliged to surrender, in the same month as the Alamo fell, he ordered them to be executed, every last man.

Sam Houston, the commander of the Texan army, was forced to retreat, and Santa Anna pursued him all the way to San Jacinto. But he was caught unawares by a clever attack

The towering San Jacinto Monument.

General Sam Houston, urging on his troops.

from a hidden position, and although heavily outnumbered, the Texans put the Mexicans to flight. It seems the Texans were hellbent on revenge, because more than six hundred Mexicans were killed, some of them as they tried to escape by swimming across a lake. Only nine Texans perished.

Santa Anna was captured, but Houston would not have him tried and executed for his crimes. He could afford to be magnanimous in victory, for the battle of San Jacinto meant the war was won and Texas had gained its independence. The nearby city was named after the man who had so bravely led the Texans. He became the first president. Ten years later the new nation became part of the United States, and went to war with Mexico yet again over a border dispute. That resulted in just under a million square miles of land being added to the United States.

The monument at San Jacinto was enormous, the tallest masonry building in the world when built, rising to a height of five hundred and seventy feet which was fifteen feet taller than the Washington monument. But then everything is big in Texas. It is America's largest state, and I was told that you could fit Britain, France, and a couple of other small European countries into Texas, and still have room to spare!

Men from Britain fought alongside the Texans at San Jacinto, a fact which is faithfully recorded in the history of the fight for independence carved in the limestone walls of the large museum at the base of the monument. Inside, an exhibition is devoted to the history of Texas, dominated by a striking portrait of Sam Houston, mounted on a horse and urging his troops forward.

It did occur to me that once again I was in a place that had witnessed a great deal of human suffering, just as in Gettysburg and Virginia. It gave me an uncomfortable feeling, and it was not to be the last time, for there was an arrangement for me to visit The Alamo.

13

Gospel Singers and a Glimpse of The Alamo

All those who know me well will readily testify, I consider music to be one of the most precious assets of life. Any kind of music will do, but a good choir, possibly a male voice choir, would certainly be among the preferred forms. So right from the beginning of the trip I remained alert for any chance to hear the essential sound, apart from jazz, of the American negro.

Gospel Singing.

Coloured people have a unique talent for music which reaches to the soul, and I would nominate Paul Robeson as one of my all-time favourite singers. I did expect to be spoiled for choice when my tour reached the Deep South, but not a hint was there in Virginia where the cottonfields once resounded to negro spirituals, if Hollywood is to be believed. And I was really taken aback when we arrived in New Orleans and attempts to locate a place where gospel music could be heard met with dismal failure. I couldn't even find a church, or any place of worship which might have a choir, anywhere in that vast shrine to music.

Paul Robeson – one of my all-time favourites.

By the time that we began to prepare to leave Houston, and aware that opportunities were rapidly diminishing, I put in a special request to my teammates, and an intensive research bid swung into action. Advice was sought from the locals, telephone directories consulted, and on the last afternoon in Houston we called at a lovely little Baptist church not far from the centre of the city which had a choir with a national

Old style Gospel Singers.

reputation. It had been selected to sing for the Queen when she visited Texas, so hopes were high.

A rather solemn senior lady, who looked every inch a gospel singer herself, surprised me somewhat by her lack of welcoming response. She was even quite dismissive of gospel singers, and it was only through the kindness of her younger assistant that we were able to obtain a list of other churches that might be able to help. A flurry of telephone calls back at the hotel established that, indeed, one church choir was performing that very night in one of Houston's open air parks – and I would be very welcome to come.

I arrived half-way through the concert because of other commitments, and there was something of a crisis in progress, because the poor organ player was being transported to hospital by ambulance. She was a lady of substantial proportions and her stool had unfortunately collapsed underneath her.

The performance went on, however, and lasted well into the night. I enjoyed what I heard, but I have to say in all honesty that the reality did not live up to expectations. Maybe the gentle old classics and the lovely spirituals that I will always associate with gospel singing are no longer in fashion. There seemed to be a political thread running through the performance, with songs like 'We Shall Overcome', and a protest recitation about trying but failing to board the 'Freedom Train'. I suppose you cannot blame them, because they clearly thought they were still an underprivileged group of people, but it was a religious occasion after all, and perhaps the political element was stressed rather too much. It would also have been better in my opinion if the volume had been turned down.

However, it was well worth the effort to track down the modern version of gospel singing, and I would have been very disappointed if I had not personally experienced it.

The next morning we drove into the very heart of Texas. There is a road called Interstate Highway Ten, which is equivalent to a British motorway, and it must be one of the most colourful routes anywhere in the world. It starts off in Louisiana and goes all the way through Texas via San Antonio and Houston to El Paso, on the border with New Mexico. That's a distance of more than two thousand miles. Once you leave Houston behind, the centre verge of Interstate Highway Ten is ablaze with wild flowers. In season, the most prominent is the blue bonnet which is deep blue and purple and the national flower of Texas, not the yellow rose as the song would have us believe. Then there is the Indian blanket, which has a brown centre, with orange, yellow and red outer leaves; and the equally extravagant Indian paintbrush, sporting red, gold, yellow and white, and occasionally I spotted red orleander bushes. All in all a real feast for the eyes, and a sight which, I was told, persuaded people to drive along Interstate Highway

The wildflowers of Texas.

Ten not to go anywhere in particular but just to view the central flower arrangements. It's easy to afford such an indulgence in America, since petrol is around one third the price that it is in Britain!

Eventually I caught sight of my first ranch and the occasional herd of cattle, which was exciting. To be frank I had expected to see a lot more cattle, but there was a reason I didn't, which was explained to me at a later date. But the sheer scope of Texas created a real impact on me. All the ranch houses were set in land which stretched for many acres, and I did hope that those who lived there appreciated all that space. I thought how pleasant it must be to raise a family in such a peaceful and uncrowded place. Such a contrast to many areas of Britain, and I just wished I could have taken a small slice of that acreage back with me to Cotherstone. Snow is a virtual stranger to Texas, which was another major attraction for me – I had my fill of snow during my sixty years and more in Baldersdale. And I was told that the temperature rarely falls below forty degrees fahrenheit.

Along the way we stopped for lunch at a small town called Luling, and I had my first taste of barbecued Texan beef. The local sheriff was eating at the next table, and a real disappointment he turned out to be. He wore a stetson and had a gun in a holster on his hip, but he looked more like an elderly assistant bank manager than Randolph Scott. Luling was an oil town and curious pumping contractions called donkeys were nodding away in the oddest places drawing up the oil. One very small one, only about five feet in height, was actually situated right alongside a garage petrol pump.

A much more attractive place was San Antonio, a city with a pronounced Mexican feel since it is situated only three hours away from the border of that country. San Antonio seems to hold a unique place in the affections of all Texans, and everyone I had spoken to in the Lone Star State on my way there said how wonderful it was. A famous Texan journalist and author wrote that 'Every Texan has two homes: his own, and San Antonio.' Regrettably, a light drizzle was falling when I arrived there and that sort of weather does tend to take the shine off any place, however appealing. I had met repeated confirmation of this truism during my tour of Europe for *Innocent Abroad*, when rain and thunderstorms pursued me all the way from Paris to Capri.

I suppose it is the Alamo as much as anything else which makes San Antonio so special to Texans. To them it is sacred ground. I found it fascinating myself, although I was aware that once again I was standing on bloodstained ground. The Alamo is situated near to the centre of the city and was originally a Spanish mission. Much of it has been destroyed, but what remains is very pleasing to the eye, since the architecture is seventeenth century Spanish and very decorative. There is, of course, a direct link between the Alamo and the battle of San Jacinto, because the Texans who defended it against the Mexicans were buying time for Sam Houston to organise an army not much more than a hundred miles away.

They held out for thirteen days, one hundred and eighty-nine men against an army of four thousand Mexicans. The heroes of the Alamo included many famous names such as Davy Crockett, Jim Bowie, the inventor of the knife named after him, plus some men from Britain. It seemed if there was a fight going anywhere, you would be fairly certain to find some of our countrymen. Eventually, Santa Anna gave the garrison a choice of either surrendering or dying, and they chose to fight to the last man. On 6 March 1836, Santa Anna's troops finally broke through the defences and slaughtered any survivors.

The Alamo is now a shrine; it is regarded as the grave of the one hundred and eighty-nine martyrs, because although Santa Anna gave his own dead a decent christian burial, he contemptuously piled the bodies of the Texans and their

The Alamo – sacred ground.

supporters into a heap and set fire to them. The place is supervised with keen discipline by a group called The Daughters of the Republic of Texas. I was given to understand that only descendants of the founders of the Republic of Texas could belong, but I did wonder why just the daughters? What happened to the sons? Anyway, the daughters obviously considered the Alamo far too hallowed to be exposed to the camera. Although tourists can wander around freely, there is a total ban on both moving and still photography. It was worse than the White House, because our camera was not even permitted on the pavement twenty-five yards away from the entrance. We had to cross to the other side of the street and try to time our shots in between the tourist buses passing between us and the Alamo.

Now I am all for showing respect, but this was making life unnecessarily difficult for people who had travelled a long way to pay tribute to the place and the men who had died so gloriously there.

But our tour then proceeded in a very convivial manner, and I was taken to a Mexican market where I walked around stalls that were selling some very exotic items, then we went on to eat at a very famous Mexican restaurant. The weather had improved dramatically after that dismal arrival, and the heat was quite ferocious during the frustrations of filming the Alamo. I was glad to sit in the shade of the restaurant's terrace and watch the sun go down.

The meal proved to be one of the most memorable of our long journey. The entire atmosphere was Mexican and filled with music and noise and extravagant personalities. I ventured a taste of Mexican food, ordering a dish called Flautos, which means flutes, and enjoyed it. It consisted of pastry cylinders stuffed with various items, and including a very palatable green concoction called guacamole. It was quite substantial for a starter and I later regretted ordering fish and chips for my main course. The restaurant specialised in Margaritas, a very famous cocktail made with a tequila base and reputed to be hazardous when given to inexperienced imbibers.

But the most satisfying part of a thoroughly enjoyable occasion was – I'm sure you will be able to guess – the music. The restaurant was a calling place for groups of wandering Mexican musicians and three of them played and sang at my table. They only had acoustic guitars and their voices to offer, but they were so accomplished that it was all they required, and they provided a lovely, romantic, conclusion to our visit to San Antonio.

Serenaded in a Mexican restaurant . . .
. . . a fruit punch, not a Margarita!
. . . and a splendid city sunset.

14

Cowboy Country – Rodeos, Longhorns and the White Wolf Dog

I finally arrived at the place Uncle Tommy so dearly wished to see. Cowboy country. They called Bandero the Cowboy Capital of Texas and it certainly looked the part, with just one dusty main street with saloons built in Western style, hitching posts for horses and even a working blacksmith.

I stayed at the Mayan Ranch just a mile or so away along a bumpy road out of Bandero. Although it wasn't a working ranch in the classic tradition, and catered very comfortably for tourists, you certainly felt as near to the cowboy life as is possible these days.

There were horses everywhere, including some highly-coloured Indian ponies of a kind I had never seen before, and everyone could ride as often as they wished. That was not for me, however, for I am the wrong age to start such a perilous activity. On the farm back home we had horses for working the fields, not as a means of personal transport. But I joined in everything else, eating cowboy-style under the trees by the river running through the ranch, with the appetite sharpened by the smell of barbecued steaks.

One evening, as I was enjoying another outdoor meal and listening to more Mexican music, I was introduced to a dog. A very extraordinary dog as it turned out. Our cameraman, Mostafa Hammuri, was the first to spot it. It was white in colour and attached to a lead held by its master, Don Hicks, the head of the family which owned the Mayan ranch.

'That is a wolf,' Mostafa said with conviction.

The Smithy – with hitching post for horses only.

HORSES ONLY

The main street of Bandero.

The blacksmith and his hat!

His assertion was ridiculed at first, but then Barry Cockcroft took a closer look and exclaimed, 'Ye Gods, I think it *is* a wolf!'

And so it was, unmistakably so, and almost pure white, similar to the species found in Alaska or some other Artic area. Mr Hicks, who described himself as the Head Wrangler of the ranch, explained to me that it was a ten-month-old bitch, and she was eighty per cent wolf and twenty per cent white German shepherd. He called her Mariah. Until the previous

Don Hicks and the white wolf dog.

year he had owned a dog which had Mariah's pedigree in reverse order – eighty per cent white German shepherd and twenty per cent wolf. It had been shot on the borders of his land, which he said had broken his heart. Being a dog lover myself I could understand his grief. So he had set out to replace his pet, and chanced to hear of a man who had a white pup for sale similar to the one he had lost. He travelled sixty miles to see it, and said he was astonished to find the man had seven wolves chained up around his premises, which he used for breeding. The pup was just six weeks old and I would guess a very rare and costly specimen, although I did not enquire how much he had paid for it. I cannot imagine how you arrange a cross with such a high proportion of an animal which has inspired fear in man for centuries. There are stories about the Big Bad Wolf which condition us from childhood, but I believe that this has given the species an entirely false reputation, and I've had it on good authority that wolves would never attack a human, unless cornered or defending their young. I know they prey on cattle, sheep and other farm animals, but so do foxes.

Outdoor dining at the Mayan Ranch, with Mexican music.

Mr Hicks said that Mariah had become a wonderful dog, settling in happily with his family and friendly to everyone, particularly children. Mariah certainly behaved like any other amiable dog, rolling over to have her tummy tickled, and nuzzling up to you when being petted. The constant turnover of visitors to the ranch bothered her not at all, and apparently the only people she barked at were salesmen! I agreed with her owner that this wasn't a bad trait – it made her even more valuable, in fact.

I then told Mr Hicks about my ambition to see cowboys in action so he said I had come to the right place. Bandero might be small, and could be referred to as a one horse town, but it had seven rodeo world champions, mostly for roping cattle, so if I wanted to see real cowboys then I would have to go to a rodeo.

In rural Texas the rodeo seems to be the major public attraction, and there are cowboys taking part who are full-time professionals earning large sums. I'm not sure if you could describe what they do as sport in the strict sense, but it is

A tense moment at the rodeo – the injured rider's girlfriend on my right (*top left*).
Roping a calf (*bottom left*).
An exceedingly dangerous occupation! (*top right*).
Conversation with an old cowboy (*bottom right*).

competitively based. There was an arena a couple of miles outside Bandero where rodeos are held every week, so I was naturally keen to go.

What I saw was a remarkable combination of real Western skills and raw courage. I thought how delighted Uncle Tommy would have been, if he could have been sitting next to me on that warm and humid night, watching the true successors of the American cowboy tradition he had admired so much in an all-action display. I considered the cattle roping competition required the sort of ability most valuable on a working ranch. The cowboys worked in pairs, racing after a calf at full gallop, whirling lariats around their heads. One had to rope the head, and the other the feet, to bring the beast to the ground. It was done against the clock, and the fastest pair won the prize.

One cowboy gave a marvellous solo display of lariat handling to music, standing on the back of his horse as he did so! That horse never moved a muscle – astonishing. Mind, I was very impressed by the behaviour of all the horses there that night; dozens of them, and every single one seemed to do exactly what was required of it, and at such speed. I was told they were called quarter horses, bred for their speed over a quarter of a mile, which is vital for working cattle. They certainly moved like lightning around the confines of the arena, and were very nimble and sure-footed on tight turns when in pursuit of a young beast, twisting and dodging to escape.

The climax of the rodeo was quite alarming, and required courage to the point of foolhardiness. Bullriding. Huge beasts of the Indian Brahma variety, those which have a hump behind their necks and were introduced to Texas to add bulk to local herds, were penned into a narrow corral. The cowboy intending to ride one had to lower himself very carefully on to its back, because the bull's protests usually threatened to burst the planks apart. When the cowboy signalled that he was ready, the gate was sprung open and the bull came tearing out, bucking furiously. The winner was the one who could stay on longest, and everyone I saw had a very uncomfortable landing indeed. They must have been a mass of bruises at the end of the ordeal.

There was one heartstopping moment when a young man was thrown almost immediately and got caught up in the bull's harness. For several agonising seconds he couldn't free himself and seemed to be badly trampled. It was made all the more nerve-wracking for me because I happened to be sitting next to his girlfriend, who had told me he was the next to ride. His colleagues raced to his aid and got the enraged bull safely away, but he remained a crumpled heap in the dust for several minutes until he slowly rose to his feet and waved to the crowd. I imagine he was signalling to his girlfriend that his injuries were not serious, and I have to say she took it all quite calmly. She saw how concerned I was and assured me that he would be all right. Apparently he had been taking part in bull riding competitions for ten years. Mind, I think she was hiding her own anxiety, trying to be tough in the Texan tradition, because she did admit later that he was still suffering from an injury sustained doing the same thing only ten days previously. I tentatively suggested that it might be time for him to quit such a dangerous pursuit, but she just smiled sadly and shook her head.

After the excitement was all over and the crowd began to drift away I had a conversation with an elderly gentleman sitting on my other side who turned out to be a retired rancher, and a world champion rodeo rider in his youth. We talked for a long time, one cattle farmer to another, and I came away with a deep desire to see the classic kind of Texan cattle.

The Longhorn

But there were problems. The old breeds had been crossed with other varieties and the images we used to see on the

A herd of Longhorns, stretching into the distance.

cinema screen of massive herds on the move across the prairies to the railhead were a thing of the past. The basic reason is down to Nature – there had been a shortage of rain for years, serious enough to force a reduction in numbers of cattle, since the grass growth was severely retarded.

My elderly friend spoke wistfully of some acquaintances of his who owned a 2,400 acre ranch in New Zealand. There they enjoyed an average of fifty inches of rain each year, so they were able to rear 10,000 sheep, 500 cows, 34 horses, 14 dogs and 300 deer! It was not possible to match that on the parched pastures of Texas.

Continuing my quest for old Texas, I went wandering in Bandero and came across a smithy I had heard about, which looked as though it hadn't changed for a century. It was a charismatic, untidy place, littered with bits of ironwork and the general bric-à-brac of an old established forge, just like the ones I recalled from my youth. The fire was being pumped to a fierce heat, and a grizzled old Texan with a wonderfully weatherbeaten face was hammering away on an anvil. Outside there was a rail labelled 'Horses Only', and above the premises was a cryptic notice: 'The Price Depends on Your Attitude!'

All in all, a reassuring sight. One of the proprietors of the forge told me the happy news that the horse was making a comeback in Texas, if only for recreational purposes, and the demand for his horseshoes was almost as high as in the good old days. He said he wished I could have been in Texas in 1986 when they turned back the clock for a while by taking five hundred wagons all around the State. They covered 3,300 miles, and took six months to do it. He was the blacksmith on the trip and had obviously relished every yard. He asked me about the quality of horses in my country and, curiously enough, wanted to know if we had any mules in Britain. I told him that I had never seen one before I came to America. He also admired my hat, because I had acquired a stetson that very day from a local store, and insisted on showing me his favourite stetson. It was exceedingly well worn, heavily stained and decorated with a broken feather, but clearly a prized object for some reason. Texans seem to have a passion for headgear.

I had heard about the smithy from Mr Hicks at the ranch, so I reckoned that he might know if there were any Longhorns within a reasonable distance that I could go and visit. A couple of telephone calls after I had put the question to him, I was on my way to the L.H.7. Ranch, tucked well away down one of

Inside the Bandero forge.

the empty side roads out of Bandero. There I met Boyd Vaughan, the manager, who drove me in his pick-up truck for a mile or so over rough country – and I finally found the Texas I had been looking for.

A herd of Longhorn cattle, roaming far into the distance.

L.H.7. Ranch had a spread of around thirteen hundred acres, carpeted by wild flowers and grazed by just under three hundred head. The herd was started by Mr Vaughan's grandfather, a conservationist who noticed that the Longhorn was vanishing from the West just like the buffalo. It was being replaced and sometimes crossbred with other breeds from Europe, such as the Hereford and the Aberdeen Angus. The Longhorn originated in Spain and was brought to America by the Spanish when they conquered vast areas of the continent. It's hard to understand why they should develop such enormous, sharply pointed horns, which can grow to five feet in length and create real problems. Mr Vaughan said they were docile creatures, but you still had to take great care when approaching them. Flies were a constant menace to cattle in Texas – I saw thousands buzzing round their heads and flanks

– so if a Longhorn was irritated and swung its head when a person was close by it could cause serious injury. They could also become caught up in fencing or barbed wire. De-horning was carried out at some ranches, but Mr Vaughan pointed out that it would destroy the basic reason for founding his herd, which was to preserve the breed, warts and all, for posterity. His family had been careful to protect the pedigree of his beasts, as they were all direct descendants of the original seven Longhorn bloodlines, and each officially certificated NOI, which meant 'No Evidence of Impurity'. All the calves on the ranch had been sired by five bulls, huge creatures with a somewhat menacing demeanour. I was pleased to hear that the senior bull, now a great grandfather and no further use because of the risk of inbreeding, had been allowed to go into peaceful retirement instead of being discarded.

It was also good to learn that Mr Vaughan's grandfather's wisdom had paid off in the material sense, because I gathered that there was a waiting list of people wishing to buy bull calves and heifers to breed for themselves. Although the Longhorn is not as efficient a beef producer as other cattle, it does yield a very superior lean meat, and demand was rising.

Like all the other spreads in Texas, the L.H.7. Ranch had been severely affected by the drought. Mr Vaughan said that he grew several acres of oats and other suitable crops to give his herd winter grazing and reduce the need to fodder them with hay. But the situation had become so bad that it was necessary sometimes to put out hay in the summer. It did rain heavily once during our ten days in Texas, but apparently it would have to pour down for months to bring the land back to something approaching normality.

Oakwilt, the tree killer.

Nature was dealing another blow to Texas because many trees, particularly in the hill country, were being affected by a fungus called Oakwilt. It forms an unpleasant grey cladding on the branches, and I saw several very sick trees near Mr Vaughan's ranch house. Some were already dead, and Mr Vaughan was trying to save the others by injecting them with a fungicide.

That very satisfying visit to the L.H.7. Ranch was my last taste of the classic American West. I departed for Dallas the next day, loathe to leave the countryside for another baking city, but happy that my prime ambition had been fulfilled. It was not quite what I expected, but that's just me – living in the past. It was depressing to see the place which had fed the

With Boyd Vaughan and his herd.

imagination of so many generations through literature and the cinema going into decline through drought and disease.

Perhaps the cowboy, like the Longhorn, has become an endangered species. How could it be otherwise when the land will not support cattle like it did? I had personal evidence of that as I travelled hundreds of miles through rural Texas. I saw thousands of acres which seemed like perfect cattle country – all empty.

I suppose it was a blessing in a way that Uncle Tommy didn't share my experience. The Longhorns and the rodeo would have pleased him, but his grand vision of the American West would have been sadly diminished.

15

Dallas, Memories of J.F.K., and I Take Flight

I said goodbye to America in Dallas. Being country bred I am not fond of cities, with certain exceptions such as London or Paris, and even then a day or two is enough for me. Like many other cities in America, Dallas has a spectacular centre which we have all seen in the opening title sequence of the popular television series. But it carries a burden. It was the place where President John F. Kennedy was brutally done to death. This spectre from the past was unexpectedly thrust at us immediately we arrived in Dallas, because we became lost in the traffic system and repeatedly passed the very spot where it happened.

It was noticeable how conversation in our vehicle was totally silenced by the experience and it was difficult to shake off the depression it created. I know you cannot hold a city responsible for the assassination, but some people considered that it was a disaster which still affects the world. Certainly, we do appear to be short of inspirational leaders these days. Anyway, it was just an unhappy fact of life – people cannot forget, and Dallas has to suffer the consequences.

Our American tour had been long and exhausting, with only one day totally clear of work in six weeks and that was on the QE2 when I had to stay in bed suffering from mal-de-mer. Now it was all over, and my companions had to busy themselves with final travel arrangements and the wearisome business of packing the television gear, which had to be placed in specified boxes to comply with customs regulations. As for me, I was weighed down with another matter.

The skyline of Dallas.

My original intention had been to go back on the QE2, but the next sailing was thirteen days away. Waiting around in America for such a long time was just not practical, because I would have needed a companion to guide me back to New York which was thousands of miles away. So the question was put to me.

Would I consider flying back home?

I pondered long and hard, but all the options I considered to try and avoid such a step proved impossible. So I agreed, much to the relief of the rest of the party. But sitting in my hotel room waiting for the hours to pass was quite an ordeal. A definite

John F. Kennedy.

shadow had been cast by a number of factors: firstly, the prospect of my very first flight in an aeroplane; secondly, the sombre thought that President Kennedy had died just a few hundred yards from the hotel; and finally a remark from one of our party when we were driving past that dreadful place that a building nearby was shaped like a coffin. I know it is silly, but things like that do tend to prey on the mind when you are in a tense and fearful mood.

British Airways appeared to be very pleased about my decision and swiftly arranged flights for the entire party. Personally I felt it only right that I should make my debut on our national airline, and I have to say that the British Airways staff took care of me with great kindness and understanding.

They fly direct from Dallas Fort Worth to London every day, but it's an afternoon departure and counting the hours during the morning naturally led to another build up of anxiety. We arrived at the airport early to avoid crowds, and because we had so much heavy gear and luggage to check in. We were granted the privilege of using the VIP lounge where I had a pot of tea – I find there is nothing better to steady the nerves, a good old-fashioned English cure-all. Incidentally, as I passed through the security check I was surprised to be asked for my walking stick, which was put through the X-ray machine with the rest of the hand luggage. I can't imagine what they expected it to contain. I was interviewed and photographed by a local journalist in the lounge, which helped to pass the time nicely. Then I was told we had to board, so I took a deep breath and proceeded as instructed. I had seen the aeroplane from the window. It was very large and had one engine stuck on top of the tail. They said it was a DC10. It even had a name – The New Forest.

We moved slowly away from the terminal and I was rather concerned by a long announcement about how to deal with an emergency, and how oxygen apparatus would automatically drop down from overhead if it proved necessary. At the time I was trying to concentrate on gathering myself together for the take-off and it didn't help at all. Anyway, Barry Cockcroft in the adjoining seat talked me through it.

I didn't like the take-off. Not that I ever expected to. Speeding along the runway was all right, but the moment when we lifted off the ground and the plane sloped upwards was frightening, for me. I relaxed a little when we finally achieved cruising height and Barry congratulated me for

Checking in at Dallas/ Fort Worth . . .

. . . and taking off!

'entering the second half of the twentieth century', as he put it.

The plane was comfortable enough and the food pleasant, but I could not rid myself of the thought that if anything should go wrong we would be entirely helpless. You do at least stand a chance if a ship starts to sink.

Then the captain talked to us on the public address system, telling us our position and what we could expect to see if we cared to look out of the window, which I rarely did because it tended to unsettle me. He also said we would shortly be climbing to 35,000 feet, that our speed was just over six hundred miles an hour and concluded by recommending that we should keep our belts fastened when in our seats because of the risk of turbulence – not a comforting thought.

Not long afterwards I was invited to join him on the flight

The captain of our aeroplane.

deck and he turned out to be a Yorkshireman, born in York and living for a time in Halifax. Captain Paul Howard was very gallant and charming, but he put me on a bit of a spot when he asked me if I was enjoying the flight. So I just said I was all right at the moment, and changed the subject to how well the ladies were taking care of me. I have to say that on the flight deck I felt no sensation of going at a terrific speed – indeed, looking through the cockpit window gave the impression that we were standing still. Captain Howard said we were five miles high and pointed out the white vapour trails of planes ahead. I think he may have sensed that I was nervous because he showed me the three computers controlling the navigation system, and said the astronauts had only one of the same kind to get to the moon. Later, he presented me with a certificate to mark my very first flight, signed by all the senior crew.

After we had eaten, Barry asked me to summarise my feelings about the trip now that it was coming to an end. Well, one thing was certain – I liked America very much and would willingly go back. I was particularly taken by all the space – there was room to breathe, so to speak, and the countryside was most appealing. When pressed to choose one place above all others, then I had to nominate Louisiana and the bayous, although Williamsburg and the Amish country ran a close joint-second, with Washington DC and New Orleans not far behind. The worst part was the railway journey from Washington to New Orleans, but I couldn't think of any place I wouldn't care to see again.

We flew through the night and I levered my seat into a reclining position and tried to get some sleep, but I was disturbed in more ways than one by a sudden announcement from Captain Howard, warning of turbulence ahead as he had previously forecast, and instructing everyone to fasten their seatbelts. The lights went on and the plane bumped a little but, thankfully, nothing dramatic happened. Just under nine hours and five thousand miles after leaving America, we put down at Gatwick airport. The landing was tolerable, although my ears suffered a bit and I could scarcely hear what people were saying. And I will not need to stress how pleased I was that it had been a very smooth and uneventful flight. Whether or not I will ever take to the skies again is something I will have to consider very seriously. Perhaps a short journey next time. But I will always prefer to sail if it is at all possible.

Home was good to see again, and all my friends and neighbours were so pleased to see me back – and quite astonished at the news that I had chosen to fly. But . . . I wish it could have gone on a bit longer. Another two or three weeks, perhaps.

I enjoyed my American experience so much that all the time I had been there I rarely knew what day of the week it was!

A short nap at a height of five miles!

Acknowledgements

Hannah Hauxwell and Barry Cockcroft offer sincere thanks to all the people who feature in this book, and for all the kindness and hospitality shown to them and the rest of the Yorkshire Television crew on their journey across America. Gratitude is also particularly owed to:

Edmund Swinglehurst, Alison Smith, Jill Weston, David Holden of Thomas Cook; Peter Gillbe of Optomen Television; Roger Katz and the staff of Hatchards; Rachel Wesson and the staff of the Mayfair Hotel; Eric Flounder of Cunard; Lindsay Frost, Andrew Graham, Herb Kritz, Elaine Mackay and Christine M. Wares of the QE2; A. Daniela Marino, Diane M. Emery and associates of the New York Division of Tourism; Erin Feeney, Philadelphia; Lucinda Hampton of the Pennsylvania Dutch Convention and Visitors Bureau; Donald Hebner III and the Park Rangers of the Gettysburg National Park; Charlotte Fenn (London) and Marilyn Brown, Washington DC; Joe Fab and the management and staff of the Belle Vue Hotel, Washington DC; Martha Steger, Sue Bland and Jack Berry of Virginia, Simone Rathlé-Enelow and the staff of the Windsor Court Hotel, New Orleans; Caroline Rathbone of Orient Express Hotels; Patti Young, Tracey Schreiber, Terry Westerfield, Lewis Hankins, Steve Spracklen of the Delta Steamboat Co. in New Orleans; Greg Guirard and friends in the Atchafalaya Basin, Louisiana; Chris Castro, Michael Kardos, Danni Sabota, Gina Romero and Anna Buehrer of the State of Texas.

Don Hicks and all the Hicks family of the Mayan Ranch, Bandero, Texas; the people and rodeo performers of Bandero, Texas; Boyd Vaughan of the LH7 Ranch, Bandero, Texas; Toby Oliver and Helen Malani of CIB Public Relations, London; Alan Solloway and Denis Fernandez of British Airways, London; John Lampl and Lilla Santullo of British Airways, New York; John Thorpe of the *Yorkshire Evening Post*.

John Fairley, Grant McKee, Sue Hamelman, Tina Leeming, Shelley Chadwick, Kathy Rooney, Vivien Green, Kiri Tunks, Kate Parkin, Cate Paterson, Cathy Schofield, Rosemary Volante and Behram Kapadia.

Photographic Credits

Mostafa Hammuri: Frontispiece, 13 (bottom), 17, 18, 19, 20, 21, 24 (top and bottom), 28, 29, 37, 41, 43, 44, 46, 47, 49, 55, 56 (top), 63, 70-1, 73, 74, 79, 90, 91, 93, 109, 113, 117, 119, 123, 124, 125, 127 (top and bottom), 128, 129, 133, 134, 135 (top and bottom), 138, 153, 154, 155 (top), 171 (bottom), 176, 177, 178 (top), 179 (bottom), 183, 185. **Barry Cockcroft:** 11, 13 (top), 14-15, 16, 23, 30, 32, 33, 34, 35, 36, 39, 40, 48, 50-1, 56 (bottom), 57, 58, 67, 68-9, 75, 77 (top and bottom), 78, 81, 82-3, 85, 86-7, 89, 94-5, 97, 100, 105, 126, 130, 131, 132, 145, 150, 156, 157, 159, 161, 162, 169, 170, 171 (top), 173, 174, 175, 181, 184, 189 (top), 190, 191. **Richard Reynolds (Courtesy Texas Dept of Commerce:** 6-7. **Alan Harbour (Courtesy Yorkshire Television):** 8. **Courtesy Cunard Line:** 27. **Chris Greaves:** 52 (top). **Courtesy Pennsylvania Dutch Convention and Travellers' Bureau:** 45, 52 (bottom), 59, 60, 61, 65. **Courtesy Virginia Division of Tourism:** 99, 102, 103 (top, bottom and margin), 107, 108, 111. **Courtesy The Museum of the Confederacy, Richmond, Virginia:** 106 (top and bottom). **Courtesy Amtrak:** 114-5, 120-1. **Greg Guirard:** 137, 140 (all), 141 (both), 143 (both), 147, 148, 149, 150-1. **Joan Craven, Rex Features Ltd:** 164. **John Launois, Camera Press:** 165. **Courtesy, Tourist Division, Texas Dept of Commerce:** 166, 167, 178 (bottom), 179 (top). **Peter Poulides, Tony Stone Images:** 187 (top). **Patrick Farley, Rex Features Ltd:** 187 (left). **Courtesy, British Airways:** 189 (middle).